WHAT PEOPLE ARE SAYING ABOUT

AVENUES OF THE HUMAN SPIRIT

A fascinating Book. Lots of people have written about their out of body experiences, but few have taken the trouble to follow through in this way. The result is an important, multi-layered work that goes far beyond the question of out-of-body experiences to present a thoughtful and intelligent examination of visions, psychic abilities and the nature of spirituality — all particularly potent for being based largely on personal experience. Avenues of the Human Spirit is a book I would recommend unreservedly.
Herbie Brennan, *New York Times* Best Selling author of more than 7.5 Million books worldwide.

Searingly honest, real and spiritually inspiring, Avenues of the Human Spirit is a fascinating journey from the personal to the universal, Nicholls' book serves as a catalyst for readers to further unlock their own spiritual potential, to break through barriers and go beyond boundaries. Carefully navigating a middle course with feet firmly on the ground, he shares direct, first hand experiences of his flights to the farther realms of consciousness. If you're looking for an indispensably inspiring, must-read account of one seeker's unique voyage of discovery to gain further understanding of the vast potentials of human consciousness... this is it. A stunningly courageous book!
Karen Ralls, Bestselling author, *The Templars and the Grail; Music and the Otherworld*

A captivating account. Blending compelling personal spiritual experiences with a modern scientifically based world-view.
Alex Tsakiris, Host of the Skeptiko parapsychology podcast

Avenues of the Human Spirit will surely achieve its goal of motivating readers to not only explore various ways to evolve spiritually, but this book will further compel readers to use their new-found spirituality to create positive social change.

Philip Paul, The Out of Body Experience Research Foundation

This is a wonderful, entertaining and unique book about remarkable out-of-the-body experiences and altered states of consciousness. Graham Nicholls brings us intelligence, wry humour and a warm heart as he describes his spiritual journey from his boyhood in a London council flat to his career as a successful artist. Most of all, he inspires us to celebrate and enjoy the wonder and magic of life.

William Bloom, author of *The Endorphin Effect, Feeling Safe and Psychic Protection*

Avenues
of the
Human Spirit

Avenues
of the
Human Spirit

Graham Nicholls

BOOKS

Winchester, UK
Washington, USA

First published by O-Books, 2011
O-Books is an imprint of John Hunt Publishing Ltd., Laurel House, Station Approach,
Alresford, Hants, SO24 9JH, UK
office1@o-books.net
www.o-books.com

For distributor details and how to order please visit the 'Ordering' section on our website.

Text copyright: Graham Nicholls 2010

ISBN: 978 1 84694 464 2

A CIP catalogue record for this book is available from the British Library.

Design: Stuart Davies

Printed in the UK by CPI Antony Rowe
Printed in the USA by Offset Paperback Mfrs, Inc

We operate a distinctive and ethical publishing philosophy in all
areas of our business, from our global network of authors to
production and worldwide distribution.

CONTENTS

Dedication

For my mother and father, whose love, unending support
and belief in me have made this book possible.

Preface

'I found myself standing on the shore looking out at the night-time ocean across the rocky coast of Sardinia. I was penniless, but I felt totally alive. The moon gleamed above me, its light reflecting on the waves like a shimmering path leading out into the unknown. A few hours before I had been transformed in a way that left me feeling connected and whole. I had seen in the frame of my memory both the hardships and the transformative moments in my life so far, the night I had been beaten by muggers as a teenager, yet at the same time I could feel the freedom and exhilaration I felt the first time I floated into the sky whilst in an out-of-body experience. I remembered the night my spiritual understanding had begun when I was no more than four or five years old, the ethereal figure standing before me like a messenger from the other side of reality. I had seen it all like in a subtle, almost indescribable, moment the universe had touched me and changed something in me forever, as surely as the haunting light of the moon would be transformed into the amber rays of dawn in a few hours' time.'
– Diary entry, July 2002

The words in this book describe moments from the first three decades of my life, a life of enquiring into the nature of our spiritual reality. Moments of reflection, struggle and pain as well as ecstasy and elation beyond my previous imaginings.

Completing this work has been a far greater challenge than I ever imagined, as the honesty and strength needed to reveal so much of myself was at times painful. I have had to challenge my belief systems, my knowledge of the world and even to abandon long held assumptions. Somehow placing words onto a page causes you to reconsider your choices and look at yourself anew. *Avenues of the Human Spirit* is the result of a sincere enquiry into the nature of spiritual experience. It is about that full range of perceptions, values and motivations we have come to understand as spirituality.

Every individual journey is unique and my own experiences only highlight that all the more. Yet they also reveal a deep connection between all of life on this planet; an understanding that direct contact with the transcendent proves to us the importance of growing from our experiences, of learning and exploring. In writing this book I have had to overcome my desire to offer black and white answers, to claim that I know how the world works; instead I have focused on a spirituality based upon the humility that we are all students of the world. Without this the limited ideas and judgements of past beliefs about our spiritual nature can arise.

Renewal and questioning are the basis of a spirituality of the future and it is that very way of viewing the world that helped me to realise this work. In fact shortly before completing work on this book I decided to undertake a journey across Europe. I think most reading this will understand the process of leaving a place behind in order to look at the everyday or familiar with fresh eyes. After packing away my possessions I headed for Helsinki, Finland as I had friends there I wanted to visit. My plan was then to head South and then West back across mainland Europe until I reached England again.

After a time in Finland, already feeling inspired, I boarded the ferry to Tallinn. Almost as soon as I saw the steeples of the Old Town I knew I'd found the place I would complete my book. I stayed for a week on that first visit and in that week met some truly beautiful and spiritual people. I listened to them play music until the early hours of the morning and held conversations on spiritual and social topics that seemed to arise from everyone I met. It was like I'd found a place bubbling over with talent and awareness. It was clear that I'd done the right thing in leaving England and exploring the possibilities that lay in unimagined places. When I did leave Tallinn I had already told the friends I'd made I would be back; I don't think many believed me at the time.

I then headed south to Riga, Latvia then on to Vilnius, Lithuania. When I arrived the streets were lined with buskers and artists, a whole array of personalities and colours. I spent my days walking through the city visiting landmarks and also trying to get away from the controlled atmosphere of the tourist areas to get a sense of what the city was really about. I met locals, made new friends and felt a sense of peace and creativity welling up as I left to continue on to Poland. As the bus pulled away from Vilnius my thoughts again turned to Tallinn and my building desire to begin writing again.

This sense of longing to write stayed with me as I continued on through Gdansk, Warsaw and then to Krakow, where I visited the sites of Auschwitz 1 and Auschwitz 2-Birkenau concentration camps. My journey to that point had been about my own desire to explore and to finish this book for my own purposes, but somehow being in Auschwitz reminded me that my plan for this book was to explore a spirituality based on growth and humanity, a real understanding of the value of life. I didn't want to write another book that was only about the author; I wanted to write something about spiritual community and freedom from hate, violence and bigotry. Auschwitz reaffirmed for me the importance of a new spirituality that at its core seeks to grow and change towards greater compassion and peace.

I then headed on to Vienna before returning to London to give a lecture at an event there. After that I saw friends and family before arranging a hostel in Tallinn and boarding a plane back to Estonia. Walking from the plane I had a clear sense of purpose and nothing to distract or limit me. Once settled I spent a few months working out of a small room, before moving to a beautiful house in the Old Town where I put the final words of this manuscript down.

As you read this book I hope that you will gain something of the process I went through in creating it, but more than that I hope that it will offer something life-affirming, something akin to coming into contact with a new culture, a new way of living or understanding the world. I hope you will read on with something of the traveller in your heart, open to unknown possibilities and horizons.

Graham Nicholls - Spring, 2010
www.grahamnicholls.com

Acknowledgements

I would like to acknowledge all those who have helped, influenced and inspired me to write this book, including those with whom I have lost contact or not mentioned here. I hope that this book will find its way into the hands of a few of those people.

I would like to thank my family and those who have been like family to me over the years, especially, Anna Rother and Carmen Sang, who have now passed on, but whose memory remains like a guiding light in my life.

I would also like to thank my friends and those who have helped shape my view of the world, rougthly in order of our meeting: Jivomir Domoustchiev, Terry Moore, Gian Piras, Gemini Verney-Dyde, Tommy Rockett, Dr. Douglas M. Baker, Eucalyptus Thompson, Cecil McGrane, Julie Bavant, Demian Cervera, Nicole Harrison, Cristovão Neto, Gabriel Faccinni, Tim Le Breuilly, Max Edwards, Flavio Zanchi, James Quarrell, Kathryn Fa, and Matthew Dennis. Thanks also to the team at O-Books and those who read the manuscript and gave endorsements prior to publication including Herbie Brennan, Karen Ralls, Alex Tsakiris, Philip Paul, and William Bloom.

Special thanks to: Jo Betts for the time we spent together as partners; Lawrence Brightman and Lynda Whall (and the members of L/OGDOS) for supporting my vision and checking my manuscript; James Stone for being a part of my early exploration of various traditions; Merlyn Roberts for being a part of so many of my journeys over the last twenty years; and also Triin Tõniste for being an inspiration throughout the final stages of my work on this manuscript.

I would also like to thank the scientists who are exploring the evidence for psi in the face of so much hostility, including: Dean Radin - Senior Scientist at the Institute of Noetic Sciences, who offered me his views on precognition and psi, and Rupert Sheldrake for allowing me to work with him on his research into telepathy.

Finally, I would like to thank those I met in Estonia during the completion of this book. Many were experiencing spiritual awakenings while I put the final words of this book onto paper and there is little doubt that the beautiful setting of the medieval city of Tallinn will remain in my heart into the future.

I

The Threshold

I was awoken by silence, an uncharacteristic stillness, as if time had been momentarily suspended. The ebb and flow of the traffic outside that normally accompanied my sleep was absent. Instead the atmosphere seemed full and heavy, almost tangible in the darkness of the room. A pressure from all sides seemed to bear down on the walls, as if trying to make them give way and allow whatever it was on the other side to enter. The energy was so powerful that it seemed as if the room was submerged in water. I felt compelled to get out of bed and go to the corridor outside my bedroom. It was not unusual for me to get up in the night as a child, but this was different.

I don't recall how I did actually get to the corridor, just that it seemed even more alive with energy. I just remember coming to a stop a metre or so from my bedroom facing the main doorway of the flat. I had stopped because in front of me stood a figure; it was too tall to be my mother or father and its eyes seemed to look deep into every part of my young consciousness. My fear made me stand motionless as this strange apparition continued to look at me, still and silent. I tried to call out to my parents but I wasn't able to produce a sound. Instead I dropped to my knees in order to gain a sense of comfort from the solidity of the floor. I pushed my fingers into the slightly coarse carpet, the sensation reassuring me on some level that I was safe and in the familiar surroundings of my home.

I looked up to find that the energy continued to flow in every direction and even the doorway in which the figure stood seemed to extend out into another place or time.

Although my fear held me to the spot, there was also a feeling that something very important and transformative was taking place. The fear came from me, not from anything the apparition had done. In fact it had more of the feeling of a messenger or guide than of anything negative. I believe it was simply my natural flight or fight instinct that was at play. The more I looked into the eyes of the tall ethereal figure the more I felt like I was being given something. Looking back now, even without appealing to mystical explanations for what took place, it is clear that I was opened to a new and life-changing avenue of enquiry in my life.

The experience finally ended with my drifting off into unconsciousness; the energies seemed to reach a peak that resulted in my losing all sense of my surroundings. I think I crossed a threshold that night in my childhood. The black and white certainties of innocence were gone, which revealed a mysterious aspect to my life in which everything was somehow changed. That experience aligned me to new possibilities; and as my experiences continued over the years into adulthood, that night became the first reference point in my life to suggest there is more to the natural world than what we know with our five senses.

At the time I was living with my mother and father in a tower block in London. The building had a tall dark exterior of brown brick, patterned with fading blue panels, much like many other 1960s buildings throughout the city. Even though it was only around a decade or so old it had already begun to show signs of disrepair. The dark grey concrete steps of the stairwells were coloured by stains that seemed to reveal their history. Each of the twenty floors were virtually identical giving little idea of the people who lived there. The whole building had the air of a place forgotten, even the outside walls and the crumbling wooden window frames seemed to struggle under the strain of the winds that would whistle around them.

Despite the grim outward appearance of the area in which I grew up my childhood was a creative and happy time on many levels. There were hardships, but most of my difficulties were to come from the realities of the street culture of London. My family life had its problems too, but my parents were and are inspirational and extremely supportive towards me. As a child my father would tell imaginative stories that he would make up as he went. They were all the more powerful for the way they came directly from his mind. My father travelled the world while in the navy before I was born and has a strong knowledge of history and places across the globe. He always encouraged me to see value in other cultures and planted the seed that inspired me to travel as I got older. Even the fact that for most of my childhood he was a dustman became an inspirational part of my early life. He would find antiques and curiosities thrown out with the rubbish; everything from the pencils I used to draw with, to the tennis rackets I played with at the weekends, were found by my father thrown away by someone, or left in a vacant home. Even sometimes valuable things such as paintings and vases would be discarded and find their way to our small flat. As a child I learnt a lot just from the things people from other walks of life would leave or throw away.

My mother has a very different character; her focus in life has always been caring for others. She was a carer for most of her working life, spending her days shopping, cleaning and generally looking after the elderly. She had my brother at a young age and had gone through some extremely difficult times earlier in her life and I think that gave her an empathy with people that cannot be gained in any other way. That sense of empathy had a similar effect on me, as my mother taught me the value of giving.

My early school life was a complex time, especially after seeing the apparition. I felt different; the world seemed somehow changed. It's hard to put the shift that I felt into words, especially when I realise I am describing myself at such a young age, but there was a sense of things being renewed, like the previous years in my life were in a darker time when I was less acutely aware. It was like my life was beginning now, like a connection to something greater had been made. I felt like there was an almost adult awareness, as if I could understand certain levels of social interaction far beyond my years. Even though that night had been the most terrifying experience I had been through, it felt necessary for me to begin to question and explore the world around me. The everyday realities of school felt like a distraction from my thoughts and the part of myself that was unfolding. It was mainly the subjects that held some sense of mystery that inspired me.

I remember my very first teacher commenting on my vocabulary being unusually well developed for such a young child. I was also extremely creative and fascinated by the way things worked; I was gifted with technology from a young age and was using a computer while still in primary school, something that was true of only a handful of others around me at that time. I was very confident about my future and believed intensely I would achieve many things later in life. Even to call it a belief might be understating it; there were many aspects of my life I expected to take place with absolute conviction. I don't know where this confidence came from but it was always there. Sometimes the process of learning felt frustrating to me as I felt somehow I should already know these things. I preferred to find my own way outside of the education system and explore the areas that mattered to me.

Yet there were some during my early schooling who inspired and fascinated me. One teacher in particular stands out, a young bearded man named Mr. Crombie who looking back now seemed to have fully embraced the spirit of the seventies. On one day in particular he showed us slides he had taken during a trip to Mexico. He described the step pyramids and the ancient culture that had built them as well as the many adventures he had had during his travels. I began to see in him a spark of inspiration that was so missing in much of the education I was receiving. He was a very peaceful and kind man unlike the more austere teachers I was used to. He helped me to learn to swim, and I remember it was his patience and kind nature that allowed me to trust him enough to swim for the first time.

Another area that seemed to relate to my changing view of the world was art. I remember a trip to the National Gallery in Trafalgar Square in central London organised by my first art teacher. Our group sat cross-legged in front of some of the world's great works of art while our teacher began to explain the myths and stories that lay behind them. The Virgin of the Rocks by Leonardo Da Vinci is one example that I remember from my childhood. In finding a deeper understanding of those works I connected to that same sense of mystery I had been feeling on some spiritual level, but here being expressed in the beauty not just of the surface of the painting but in a sense of the timelessness of the ideas beyond. I believe in some sense I saw in those moments the sublime meaning that those paintings were created to convey. After all most were not originally created to hang on the wall of a gallery, but were designed to immerse a religious believer in a state of reverie.

As my teacher explained every facet of a work's creation I

would become more and more focused and attentive to every word, be it to a description of the paint being made from a precious stone ground to a powder, or to the grand classical mythology the artist presented on the canvas through those same pigments. In each detail the painting became more alive. I recall in particular a painting called The Wilton Diptych, a gilt-framed painting of the Virgin Mary surrounded by angels realised in vivid blue, a pigment made from the semi-precious stone Lapis Lazuli. Some of those inspiring details have stayed with me my whole life.

During my childhood Turner's Fighting Téméraire, a depiction of a legendary ship being towed to the scrapyard to be destroyed, also captivated me; it seemed to encapsulate the specific energy of London. I have always felt a special connection to that painting, and art in general seemed to hold something of the key to things for me.

Other subjects such as the history of battles and of kings and queens left me cold, yet when the subject shifted to cultures with a mystical focus I was captivated. The ancient world such as China, Egypt, Greece, the Native Americans and many others including prehistoric Britain, held something that I could relate to on a deeper level.

I was beginning to expand my focus beyond the stereotypes of how someone from a housing estate and working class background is often expected to be. While the other children played games based on television programmes they had watched the night before, I was drawn to the folklore in children's stories or to creating games based around nature, such as a fruit tree that grew in the playground or the life cycles of the small creatures going on in the rose-beds that lined the outer edge of the concrete playground. Yet despite these inspirational elements to my childhood my differences also made me stand out. I would often find myself frustrated with those around me and this would result in conflict. One incident in which I refused to carry out the order of an adult resulted in her physically grabbing me; a struggle ensued, after which I was suspended from school. I was suspicious towards authority after that, and much of my time at school became overshadowed by problems.

As I got a little older and started to attend secondary school things did not improve. The education system was in a bad way, resources being extremely scarce. The street culture of London began to take over, and I became involved in the harsher side of London life.

It became clear that both the everyday hardships and challenges of life were as much a part of my learning as my mystical perceptions. Looking back I can see that the sum total of my experiences was the basis of a steady transformative process, a personal or spiritual evolution. I have gradually come to a realisation that this process is a form of natural initiation or rite of passage. Not the kind of initiation that we often think of as a prescribed ritual, but an initiation that takes place through life's shifts of understanding. Each experience in our lives becomes a step towards a spiritual maturity. I do not see this evolution as having a prescribed ultimate destination, but more a sense of becoming spiritually attuned. It is a process of realising, simply and intuitively, our potential in life.

As I reached twelve years old my early childhood experiences had begun to develop into unusual insights and perceptions. This first took the form of what I would describe as precursors to what would later become full out-of-body experiences.

I began to have subtle visionary perceptions of floating a few feet above the ground; these strange experiences felt almost like reliving a memory that had never actually happened. I would wake from sleep to find myself able to perceive cloud and sky above me, as if I was somehow seeing through walls. These perceptions would last for a few brief moments before I would find myself looking at the familiar setting of my bedroom again.

I had always had connections to places and things, as if I had somehow seen them before in another time or knew things I could not have been aware of on a conscious level, but this awareness was vague and hard to pin down. What was happening now was much more tangible, and therefore much more challenging to my sense of things. What had seemed like an alternative perception of the world that many put down to a strong childhood imagination was now beginning to become a major driving force in my life, something that could no longer be dismissed as simply the product of a creative mind.

I remember pulling an old battered astrology book from my father's shelf. He had never really read it; it was just another curiosity he had salvaged while clearing the forgotten debris of a vacant home. Its large purple cover and colourful illustrations were captivating, but while they inspired my imagination they held no real clue towards understanding what had been happening to me. My mother and father having little interest in religion or mysticism had no other books on anything 'metaphysical'. I would simply have to seek out that knowledge elsewhere. Nevertheless I studied that old book, especially the elaborate pictures and planetary symbols that decorated every page. I didn't really know why, I was just feeling my way in the dark.

Over the coming weeks and months I watched anything on television to do with extra-sensory perception or the so-called supernatural. I read magazine and newspaper articles; sadly most were tabloid in style, but they did at least offer an avenue for me to gain a little more understanding of alternative termi-nology, as well as some new areas to explore.

It was around a year later that I walked down the steps of a bookshop on James Street, close to the busy shops and tourist attractions of Oxford Street in the centre of London. My intuition and curiosity had finally drawn me to try and find out more about my experiences. The shop had very little, but on a high shelf almost on its own, I found a small book entitled *'Out of Body*

Experiences: A Handbook' by Janet Lee Mitchell. I remember the anticipation as I rushed home with that small book under my arm. I sensed that this was the start of something life-changing, yet at the time I had no idea of what it would entail.

2

Stepping beyond the body

It was early evening in October and already dark. This transitional time of year always has a comforting feeling about it for me. But this sense of comfort also marked a feeling of failure. For six months I had stretched out on my bed, cleared my mind and relaxed in an attempt to induce an out-of-body experience. I was almost at the point of giving up. Yet on this particular evening something was different

I had not been lying there long when an almost violent surge shot through my body like all the effort of the previous months had built up into a single transformative moment. I opened my eyes to the realisation that I was floating above my body like a translucent reflection of myself. Currents of energy seemed to pulse and flow throughout my shimmering form, and although I could barely move, and only side-to-side as if a pole extended from my head to my feet, the intensity of what was happening gave me a deep sense of freedom. I had finally achieved what I set out to do months before.

To achieve that first consciously induced out-of-body experience I had spent night after night going through complex visualisations, ranging from imagining I was floating to extending my perception to another point in space. I had pieced together some techniques from notes in the back pages of the book I had bought. Most nights I would just find myself drifting into strange half asleep, half awake states, in which my mind simply wandered. Sometimes I would drift off into sleep altogether, which I now know is common when going through these kinds of techniques; but I was determined not to give up.

When I finally succeeded and found myself looking down at my motionless body lying below in that first induced experience I remember vividly the image of my body. It appeared almost grey and still and reminded me of the appearance of a black and white photograph. Almost like a part of the environment in which it lay; it appeared stony, almost statuesque. My 'second' body was luminous and radiating, which seemed to add a slight hue to the room. The experience lasted only a few moments, but confirmed the path I was beginning to tread.

In the weeks and months that followed I would lie on my bed on my back with my hands by my side just as I had seen in illustrations and read in descriptions of out-of-body experiences in the various books that I had by now accumulated. My awareness would flow through different states in which I would lose perception of time. I would often find myself in a calm, still state in which my mind was infused with light, like I was lying in the intense rays of the sun. When I did succeed in fully projecting it was often with little or no control and usually after hours of effort. Fear was often present, but also a sense of excitement and fascination. I was entering a new world of possibility and that was more powerful than any sense of foreboding.

The hardest fact of all was that I could not move freely in the manner I had read so much about. I felt heavy and slightly oppressed, like I was carrying heavy weights. Fatigue often set in and I would find myself back in my body. This went on for some time before I gradually began to gain a greater sense of comfort through experience. I began to find that with practice I could move in a particular direction if I used a sufficiently high degree of concentration. It reminded me of swimming in the sea; tides of energy would push or pull me in a certain angle like a current or tide. I realised that I needed to work 'with' these tides and also avoid being distracted in any way if I was to progress. I found that I could compensate for the angle of the energy flow, much like a swimmer might use more force on one side or alter their technique to compensate for a current. This 'compensation' soon became second nature and I started to look toward taking my explorations further.

These early out-of-body experiences were often limited to the boundary of my home. I found that my journeys were restricted to some extent by the areas I was familiar with. I could move through doors and even walls with relative ease. I remember very early on being fascinated by the feeling of placing my hand, or what seemed like my hand, into a solid object, but the outer boundary of my flat seemed another matter. I'm sure it was to do with my own limitations and fears; the outside world was, after all, not as safe as the familiar and everyday world of my home. Even the fact that gravity and distance had little meaning in this state was overwhelming.

Actually leaving my home whilst in my *second body* was an intense process. The first time I consciously did it was like pushing through a wall of energy; like a pressure or force was repelling me and preventing me from moving forward, much like trying to push two opposing magnets together. It took a force of will to push through until I finally felt the pressure release and a new sense of freedom fill me with excitement. I had probably moved no more than a few feet, but I had overcome a major barrier, and the further I moved the freer I seemed to become.

Once outside my home, the mundane objects that in everyday life seemed almost invisible, the dull concrete and metal structures that make up the city would now sometimes take on strange energetic patterns, colours and vibrations.

I recall one event in which I became aware of being maybe a few hundred metres from home, not far from the secondary school that I was still attending at the time. I was floating vertically at a height equal to the tops of the lampposts, a height that would be consistent with many of my experiences. I remember looking at the trees around me; the organic objects looked different to their physical appearance and seemed like they were vibrating on a subtler frequency to that of the concrete and glass. The denser stationary objects, like buildings and parked cars, seemed to have taken on the energy of the activities around them, which reminded me of the way that metal begins to glow as it heats up. They seemed almost more energised than the living things, the plants and trees. This seemed opposite to what I would have assumed would be the case. I remember thinking, "surely living things would radiate more than a block of concrete".

I would later find that I would sometimes be more and sometimes less attuned to this organic frequency. Sometimes living things would seem almost unbearably luminescent, while at other times they would appear dull and almost invisible to me.

It seems common that those who have these experiences often describe a similar sense of vibration and frequency to what I have experienced, and the type and level of success with these experiences is dependent upon some kind of understanding of these shifting frequencies.

As I read more and more on out-of-body experiences it became clear that with greater experience and understanding I should be able to push myself to more distant locations than I had so far. Several books recommended meditation as a way of developing on many levels so I began to experiment with breathing practices such as pranayama, an ancient yogic system of breathing. Prana is a vital energy, believed to sustain all life and to flow through channels in the body. The belief is also that this energy can be cultivated through training the way that we breathe.

I also undertook the practice of stilling the mind; I began to learn how to enter a state of no thought or no mind. After many months of diligent practice I found that although this practice had profound implications on a spiritual level, it activated a different part of myself to the one I was trying to access.

I noticed that pranayama and sharp breathing processes did allow me to access greater levels of energy and explore the out-of-body state for longer periods and also to travel further. I was beginning to discover there was a clear relationship to the way in which we breathe.

Physical energy levels were also important in different forms; one particularly memorable experience taught me that being physically exhausted from exercise or other physical exertion was an ideal condition in which to have an OBE, as the body wants to rest but the mind is invigorated and alert from the body's activity.

The experience began with a trip to the New Forest, an ancient area of woodland in the south-east of England. We had spent the day travelling around the heathland populated by roaming horses and characterised by colourful heather. The day had been long and we had walked and driven for many miles. It was dark by the time we arrived back home and I finally had the opportunity to stretch out on my bed; within seconds I felt very peaceful and ready to drift in and out of sleep for a few hours, but instead I sensed waves of energy flowing through me and a weightless feeling beginning to grow from deep inside my solar plexus. I knew that this meant I was about to have an out-of-body experience, and sure enough the waves of energy grew until I felt myself lift into the air with a sense of release and exhilaration.

As I lifted into the air I began to open my non-physical eyes only to witness the most vivid and intense colour cascading around me. As I became used to the intensity of the scene I could make out trees and countryside with a level of detail that my physical eyes had never achieved. I had somehow been drawn back to the site I had spent the day exploring, but now my engagement and connection with the place seemed on another level altogether.

The leaves of plants seemed to glisten with light and as I focused on their surface my eyes seemed to look deep into them giving a sense of the life and fertility flowing through their delicate structures, as well as flowing through the land they were intimately connected to.

I felt ecstatic travelling over the treetops with a sense of total peace and freedom; everything was alive and transfused with light. I simply went with the experience and felt charged and revitalised by the beauty that passed by as I viewed the landscape from my non-physical vantage point.

I do not really recall how long the experience lasted that evening, but I do remember opening my eyes back in my body with an awesome sense of peace and joy. The resistance and heavy sensations I had experienced years earlier had dissolved away; fear had been replaced with an ecstatic sense of bliss and freedom. However, this sense of freedom was also blurring my sense of time. I was beginning to find that I was losing sense of how long an experience was lasting, with no real way to under-stand why. Most experiences would last around twenty minutes, but sometimes I was unable to maintain any sense of the time I had spent exteriorised.

In one experience I lost a whole twelve hours; it seemed to me as if I had been in the state for only an hour or so. I don't know if the experience actually lasted twelve hours; it was more likely that I had drifted into a kind of deep trance state in which time had simply washed over me. This kind of experience made it clearer and clearer that I was becoming increasingly immersed in the experiences. I was accessing deeper and deeper levels of consciousness.

Strange energies were often apparent within deeper experiences and I would encounter what seemed like other levels of reality. I remember lifting out of my body into an awe-inspiring fountain of light that seemed to extend over a huge area; it seemed like I had entered another world in which thoughts or mind were one. There was a sense in all this that I was encountering something of the true nature of this out-of-body reality, or what has been described as the *'astral planes'*, or the *'Locales'* in the writings of Robert Monroe[1]. This strange reality seemed like a kind of collective or even quantum consciousness. As the experience continued I felt myself lifted up into the stream of energy and felt like my mind was operating through complex patterns of thought much larger than my brain, allowing me to apprehend concepts and ideas far beyond my everyday level of learning or understanding.

A powerful fact about these new deeper experiences was that I found that in some instances I would be able to perceive things outside of what my normal senses were capable of, which obviously challenges the idea that OBEs are no more than hallucinations.

The earliest example I can recall was a normal evening; I lay down with the intention of inducing an OBE and went through a technique in which I would try to project my consciousness to a point in the far corner of the room. Within moments I found myself in a part of London, near to Paddington Station, I had not been to for some time. As I moved down to street level I focused in on an 'A' sign, the kind that lists the day's specials outside a restaurant. I realised I could read the details listed. Almost as suddenly as it had begun the experience was over. I sat up with the image of the sign still vivid in my mind; I knew I had to go there and see if the sign did indeed read as I had seen it. The excitement filled me with adrenaline when I found that the sign was as I'd seen it in the OBE down to the colour of the paint and position in the street. At that time I had several more occurrences like that, but as you will see later these were only the beginning.

These experiences took me into the realm of objectivity and opened up all sorts of difficult questions. These objective experiences gave me at least an insight into a possible answer to one of these questions, the most common question I am asked: *"But is it real, how can you be sure it wasn't just a hallucination or dream?"* This is an inevitable and understandable question. But the experiences I have had answer that question with as much certainty and integrity as I could offer. It is a question I have asked myself countless times along the path to gaining some understanding of these experiences. It is not a question I have taken lightly, and I do believe in life it is important to keep in mind the possibility you could be wrong. But when I weigh up the anecdotal, scientific and personal evidence it seems to me there must be something taking place at a level that at this point in history we do not fully understand.

Over the years I have had many discussions with those critical of the possibility of any form of 'psi'[2;] the most common argument I have heard to explain away objective experiences, in which accurate information outside of normal sensory perception is obtained, is that a cognitive bias such as *confirmation bias* took place. Confirmation bias suggests that we interpret information that confirms our preconceptions; essentially we unconsciously make things fit after the fact. Although I'm sure this does take place and I would go as far as to say this is probably quite common; it seems lacking as an explanation to really account for the depth, accuracy and complexity of these often life changing experiences. If I apply this suggestion to my own more objective experiences, experiences that I will discuss in more depth later, it does not add up as an explanation. I have kept detailed diaries since I was fourteen years old, and often the information that has come from an OBE has been far beyond any simple coincidence or bias.

This I know is the case with many others, and not just in the realm of anecdotes and personal experience, but within the world of science as it stands as well.

An in-depth discussion of the science involved is beyond the scope of this book; but what is interesting is that there are many now within the science community who are not dismissing seemingly non-physical experiences, or the evidence that has been amassed within the discipline of parapsychology since at least 1882, with the founding of the *Society for Psychical Research* in London. There are even those, including for example Nobel laureate Brian Josephson, who have put forward theoretical models for psi functioning based on their understanding of Quantum physics.

The earliest theory I am aware of relating to out-of-body experiences is the theory that the *energetic body* experienced by many may be made up of some form of subatomic particle. This idea was popularised by Sylvan Muldoon and Hereward Carrington in their 1951 book '*The Phenomena of Astral Projection*'. Sylvan Muldoon at the time was probably the most famous exponent of astral projection and his book entitled the '*Projection of the Astral Body*' is still a classic of its type.

In more recent times the theory of a kind of *phasing consciousness* that is more in line with the concept of psi has become popular. In this concept the need for an astral or energy body is less important as it is the structure of consciousness that creates the form which the experiences take. The implication is that we may be able to extend our consciousness without the literal movement of a second body. Our sensory abilities are extended via a kind of *non-local* or *quantum entanglement* in order to perceive at a distance.

The idea that the brain has been important in psychical experiences is also not new. The pineal gland, a small gland at the centre of the brain, was and still is in some circles seen as the prime candidate for the seat of the 'third eye'. The third eye is often depicted in art as being located between the eyebrows or in the centre of the forehead. Adherents of many esoteric, occult and yogic schools of thought consider it the source of psychical ability.

From a more scientific perspective a recent study of famous artist and psychic Ingo Swann[3] revealed activity in the right hemisphere of his brain when he was able to produce objective extra-sensory information. There is, however, one key area in which the idea that psi is simply a function of the brain becomes problematic, the near-death experience. These experiences classically involve an individual dying on the operating table, leaving their body and perceiving their own resuscitation from a vantage point often near the ceiling of the operating theatre. Sometimes the person who has died even perceives things outside of the room, building or even city in which their body is located. If the brain is no longer functioning, how can it be hallucinating or utilising a purely brain based faculty? The more I have explored these questions the more it becomes apparent that the answer is not a simple matter of true or false, right or wrong; it is a matter of exploration and enquiry that is likely to last a lifetime.

Whether we choose to view psychical experiences in light of a mystical tradition or within the framework of science, or even somewhere in between, I view the reality or state we access in these extrasensory experiences as the basis of a change in the way we use and define our consciousness. As we start to access a 'collective consciousness', a sense of connectedness to others and the world, this over time, and depending upon the depth of the connection that is cultivated, can grow into a sense of harmony or unity. What I am starting to outline is that spirituality can be the resulting condition of these deep psychical shifts. They can offer us an awareness of the interconnected nature of all life and the material from which life developed.

Interconnectedness

I opened my eyes to a gleaming expanse of colour and light. The most beautiful imagery revealed itself in geometric streams of light and pattern, a sunset overflowing with rich turquoise and edged by delicate pink transformed into dancing rays like the charged particles of the northern lights. In every direction a new vision of natural beauty arose. As I looked deeper into the expanse I became aware that these colours and mists of energy were the result of consciousness all around me, like I was floating in a collective mind. In each moment I became more aware of exquisite points of light mixed within waves of colour and space. I felt that I could reach out and connect with anyone, anywhere.

From the centre of the expanse rose a vast concentration of light; it was the source of all that was flowing around and it seemed to be drawing me closer to it. I felt like I was surrendering to the desire to connect with this endless sea of thought. As I touched the column of energy I rose up in a spiral of consciousness like I could think with a million minds at once. As if I was present in places all across the globe, all the emotions that characterise humanity phased in before dissolving away again. In that single moment I was consumed by the sense of endless interconnected minds. I saw the intricate lives of people across vast distances; I felt in the most tangible way the common humanity between people. No self, no separation, no now and no tomorrow. That was how I felt; accepted and totally free.

When I look back now it seems apparent that the interconnectedness I felt during that experience characterises much of psychic literature, especially when related to out-of-body and near-death experiences. These experiences happen for a complex array of reasons, in my view because these experiences are innate human faculties. They come to the fore at times of extreme emotion, often such as an illness or accident. They can also become apparent at times of lucidity and insight, times when we are 'heightened', when we are functioning at our fullest potential. They happen because they are ultimately natural aspects of life; they are simply part of our spiritual tapestry; they lead us to a greater sense of things, and a wider appreciation of the universe in which we live.

For many, out-of-body experiences, like near-death experiences, also lead to a freedom from the fear of death and a revitalised sense of purpose in life. These experiences offer a confidence that, at the very least, consciousness stretches much further than we may have believed prior.

All psychical experiences offer us the possibility that the human mind, consciousness or some form of energetic body can extend beyond the normal boundaries of what we commonly believe is possible. This is their true power; even beyond the obvious fascination that the experience itself holds, an out-of-body experience can change the way we view the world around us directly, without appeal to any philosophy or dogma.

My own experiences by my late teens had begun to give me a sense of 'interconnectedness'. This was not an intellectual knowledge or conviction; this was a sense that resulted in inspiration, and a deep feeling of confidence and stability.

Many of my experiences involved a light or energy of a quality many describe at the brink of death in a near-death experience, a light that has filled them with a sense of compassion, love and joy. This 'white light' is very important to an understanding of the link between the psychical experience and what we call the spiritual.

The term 'spiritual' is generally seen as a combination of belief, morality and self-improvement, while the psychical is often seen as more questionable within our secular societies. But for me these psychical experiences, a term into which the out-of-body and near-death no doubt fall, step beyond the common stigma they hold when we begin to look closely at the deep relationship they have to changes in the lives of those who experience them. The light, compassion and love that many encounter in these types of experiences have many effects; the most relevant to a wider spiritual viewpoint is this deep feeling of oneness. I view interconnectedness as a sense that all things have an underlying source at some level, a view that can lead to greater compassion towards others and even other forms of life. It is not through a philosophical change that spirituality truly grows, it is through direct contact with something greater than we could imagine before.

Interconnectedness is an understanding that begins with something like a vision, OBE or even a traumatic experience, something outside of our comprehension, something that pushes us to let go of our preconceptions. I believe that all development should start at the core level, the values and beliefs that are consistent across all cultures. These values include, nearly without exception, a belief in oneness or non-separateness and a sense of another level to consciousness or spirit. We lay the foundations of growth by examining the subtle lessons that we encounter through the act of living. That is why I have focused on direct experiences in the beginning of this book; I feel they offer insights into how growth takes place, how we go from something 'metaphysical' or 'psychical' to something human and profoundly spiritual. As I have mentioned, the psychical is often demeaned in secular cultures due to unscrupulous individuals and over commercialisation, but the psychical aspect of life is the foundation of most, if not all, religions and beliefs that focus directly on benevolence and charity. It is my belief that without these direct connections to our own inner teachers whom we meet in the fabric of unusual experiences, we cannot gain that real sense of possibility. That sense I call spirituality.

3

The Sphere

As my friend Gian sat ready for our meditation, I went about creating a serene atmosphere with music and lighting. I put on the music of Manuel Cardoso; beautiful layered choral harmonies I had come across a few weeks before, and placed a beeswax candle on a small altar-like area I had made. I then took my place next to him and we began to relax and focus. The sounds of the busy city outside seemed to disappear and I felt totally present in that moment, totally free from the day-to-day thoughts of the outside world. As time passed, our minds still and peaceful, the atmosphere began to heighten, like watching the light begin to appear as the sun lifts above the horizon at dawn. A delicate blue haze seemed to pervade the room, bringing with it an unusual sense of connection and awareness. An awareness that gave the subtle impression I was sitting in a place almost outside of time.

I began to glance around the room and then up towards the

ceiling; as I did I saw a large ball of green energy begin to appear above me. It glistened with a light that seemed to come from within its core. As I watched transfixed it began to slowly descend to eye level, and in so doing seemed to make some kind of connection with us, like it was conscious and aware of our presence. I glanced to Gian and he confirmed he was also seeing it. I felt calm and sensed its nature was extremely benevolent.

I sat for some time watching the glistening sphere, observing and wondering what it was and from where it may have originated, before it finally disappeared in much the same way it had come, leaving a lasting sense of presence. Gian and I were connected in a new way and it was clear we would both be defined by this mysterious level to reality that seemed day-after-day to be seeping into our everyday world.

That experience with the sphere left me wanting answers even more; it pushed me to continue to explore. This was not simply my experience; it was a shared encounter with something totally 'other'.

This opened up a world of questions. I think I was too immature to really engage fully with the implications of those questions at the time, the implications of apparitions and out-of-body experiences. Yet I was reading more and more and learning the ideas of others. It was the real beginning of my learning and by studying alternative and esoteric literature I was coming into contact with scholars in a range of subjects outside of the mystical areas I had set out to explore. I was beginning a form of education that would lead me to some of the deepest philosophical questions on the nature of existence.

I remember seeking out information within the realm of religion, but without being convinced by any one ideology. I would spend a day flicking through the pages of Lao Tzu's simple yet profound writings on the Tao. On another day I would be reading the rituals of paganism. I was uncovering a whole world of possibilities, some outlandish and some that left a lasting impression. I was beginning to realise that there was a spiritually transcendent side to my experiences, a sense of the infinite or the source of everything around us. I was hungry for knowledge; every new book I read and lecture I attended seemed to lead me closer to that something beyond ourselves, yet somehow still at our core. Something that we still don't have an adequate word to describe.

Most books on psychical topics at least imply a sense of spirituality or personal development; some go further and say that the psychical level is the first step. Then some of the more traditional religions and philosophies seem to imply that psychic faculties come to the fore with spiritual progression. And yet others still condemn these abilities as evil or wrong. There are many differing views, yet it seems that these abilities have much in common with creative flair or other natural aptitude. Many of these abilities resemble those described as the Siddhis in the Eastern philosophies; but again there seem differing views in the East as to their nature and purpose. In the West, there are many descriptions of saints or other spiritual individuals having strange powers that seem to resemble the psychic abilities of parapsychology. There seem to be two major ideas about people with these abilities within wider culture. On the one hand we have the saintly figure, connected and spiritually removed from the mundane dealings of normal people and on the other the almost opposite image of someone engaged and empathic able to connect with others through the emotional bond they are able to form with virtual strangers.

Neither of these views seemed to fit with my world view; I was not a spiritually advanced person; I was just a simple person from a very humble background. I was not particularly empathic either. Yet I did have a driving desire to understand my nature and my spiritual purpose, if I did indeed have one. All these ideas about psychic and spiritual understanding seemed fascinating, yet alien. I was from the inner city; what did all this mean in context to me?

I did not want to leave behind my sense of identity, the inner city realities of life; I felt they made me who I was. Did I really want to transcend the self, the pleasures of the senses? I meet many people who resist exploring the spiritual level of themselves as we all fear separating ourselves out, becoming alienated and unable to be a part of the world and community we love. I understand their fear as it was exactly the struggle I was going through as I developed my understanding.

It took me a long time to realise that learning and growing do not mean giving up who we are. When we were children we had one idea of the way the world is; as an adult we see things through different, but at the same time, the same eyes. Spiritual development is the same in my view; we mature and in that maturity we transcend the needs of the past by realising we are what we need to be and change takes place naturally; it is only ever a matter of what direction that change will take you in. The exact form which our personal happiness and contribution to the world will take is always dependent upon context.

For me with a background in the inner city, the spiritual tools and the ideas I can offer are limited and at the same time given strength by my background. If I had grown up in an idyllic country setting the views and ideas I could offer would be different.

When we think of the great figures of religious texts, such as Buddha or Jesus, the context of their environment is hugely important. If Siddhartha Gautama, the Buddha, had not been born a prince his view of poverty and suffering would have been totally different. Imagine Jesus not living as a carpenter, and in a world away from the power of the Roman Empire. Our environment defines our strengths and the spiritual direction or purpose we will take, be that the grand lives of spiritual teachers of the major religions or the everyday lives of normal people.

Great teachers rise up out of the context of their time and their environment. I have often been inspired by the idea that new teachers must come to the fore; it is an evolving process. Just like spirituality itself, things must change and old ideas must die and be reborn in a new form and teacher. You could look at this like a whole culture or religion being reincarnated in the body of another time.

The teacher or mentor is a recurring theme in mythological and religious narratives describing the journey of the young neophyte, from a state of innocence or naivety to maturity and understanding. In these stories there is an understanding that the mentor will have the answers for us presented through the timeless wisdom of an elder. We seek in their wise counsel a map of the territory we are about to cross. The teacher is also a symbol of our ego. Many in the West especially struggle with the idea of giving over trust and control to a teacher. We are rightly sceptical of power and patriarchal forces; yet on the other hand it is important for us to let go of our need to feel totally in control. It is also important to become aware that we do not know every-thing and that by offering our respect and concentration to a teacher we may gain something of their knowledge and experience.

This path is not for everyone and in fact for some going it alone is the only way their nature will allow. They will gain their teaching through hardships and mistakes. In some ways these people may need more than anyone to allow themselves to be guided, but may never be able to let go enough for that to become a reality. This can also be the case on the opposite side of things; the person who is too readily led may need to go it alone to find their own way in life. In that sense the teacher is also a metaphor for our own journey; the person who submits to a teacher will one day need to face their most important trials alone, and ultimately take the role of the teacher themselves. The best teachers prepare us for these trials; they raise our awareness in preparation. They help us to understand our own journey, rather than simply trying to align us to theirs. They understand that we represent the next generation, a new understanding about to come to fruition in the world.

I have encountered many teachers during my life, most not in the places we might expect but in people we encounter as we go about our normal daily activities. In the subtle lesson of a woman giving up her seat on the bus and reminding us in doing so to be aware of others, or the more emotional lessons that take the form of a passionate debate with a friend in which we adamantly resist their view before finding ourselves repeating their very words some time in the future. We have all grown and changed by our interactions whether through literally observing the actions of another or through the act of realising over time that we were wrong.

But there are also the teachers who have spent a lifetime exploring what it is to be spiritual, to live a fulfilled and expansive life. It was obvious from the reading I was doing and questions that had arisen that a teacher would be of benefit to give direction to my ideas. The first such individual I came into contact with was Dr. Douglas Baker whom I met shortly after my first induced out-of-body experiences. His spiritual path began in the worst of environments, in a war zone; he was severely injured and found himself near death. He had an out-of-body experience, which eventually led him to Theosophy and other esoteric teachings. He was the first author and speaker I ever met, and for that reason he was an important early influence. I met him after one of his lectures on astral projection and man's latent powers, as he referred to them. He seemed to come along just at the right moment for me. I began to attend his lectures on a regular basis and got to know him as a person. Although I didn't agree with all he said and indeed still don't, he offered such a range of ideas that were so available, I was able to form a solid foundation in the perspectives of a very prolific author and lecturer. In fact even at that time he had written over a hundred books and travelled the world lecturing.

One evening I set off for a lecture Dr. Baker was holding at a venue in central London. He would often sit in his car outside the venue and we would sit together and discuss ideas; looking back on it he would even test me a little to gauge if I had developed since he last saw me. On this particular evening as we walked back down the stairs together I related a plan I had been developing to start a spiritual development group. As we found our seats a friend remarked how ideal the space would be for our meetings. Dr. Baker started to pace from side to side in his familiar style and he began, *"The subject we are concerned with today, is the startling phenomena of astral projection..."*. He covered all aspects of his view of the subtle bodies of mankind and then began to relate his technique for achieving the experience. After the lecture I waited for the crowd to disperse and went over to talk with him, I asked his advice on finding a location for my group and he suggested the 'Society of Friends' or the Quakers who may offer me a room for ten pounds, as long as we made it clear we were a non-profit making organisation. He then smiled warmly and handed me ten pounds, *"That's for your first meeting"* he said.

I started to hold meetings wherever I could after that. It was still difficult as we were so young, and I recall how my age would frustrate me at the time as it was hard to be taken seriously. Also having little income was a problem so hiring halls to meet was mostly out of reach. However, I did begin working for Dr. Baker at the weekends when he needed someone to help set up the lectures. He would phone me up a few days before and I would meet him at locations across London and set up tables, chairs and also help with selling books. He would pay me in cash at the end of the meeting, and often more than I would have got for a full day's work at the time.

It was a very inspiring time in my learning; I was gaining knowledge at an extremely fast rate. My experiences too were increasing the more I focused on them. Even my friends were being impacted by my growing knowledge and awareness. I began to have experiences with others and especially close friends.

One of those friends was called Jivomir and I would eventually teach him some of the techniques that I had developed or been taught. I had been friends with him since primary school, when he had arrived from Bulgaria unable to speak English, yet somehow we communicated without words through the language of childhood. As his English grew and we became closer it was clear that we were going to share an important part of our history. After primary school we went to the same secondary school, and due to the fact we were already close, we began to explore the out-of-body state together. I remember we both noticed that our energy levels grew as we spent more time in this altered state of consciousness. I remember walking to school one morning after a night of out-of-body journeying to find myself overwhelmed by surging energy and a desire to run and move. It was like I was revitalised every time I left my body. To this day there is a powerful sense of release and energy whenever I experience this state. It is like the excited feelings we experience when visiting a new country for the first time, the heady, dizzying sense of exploration and of the new and unknown.

Jivomir worked with me setting up chairs and generally helping out Dr. Baker when he was lecturing in London. Most of our spare time was to be devoted to exploring the many approaches to the world of the spiritual or non-physical.

I felt completely connected to my experiences and what they represented in my life now. Although I did not understand them and had no idea if I ever would, I had found a focus in life and a wider community in which to express myself. The fear I had felt as a child seeing the apparition in my doorway was gone; these experiences filled me with wonder now, not dread.

A single fleeting experience can be rationalised and even dismissed, but year after year of unusual perceptions results, for most, in either the acceptance of a particular ideology, such as a religion or spiritual philosophy, or an enquiry into possible explanations in the context of science and reason. What I envisioned, and still do, is some kind of enquiry into the strengths and lessons in both. This approach seemed to offer greater insights into my experiences than simply accepting the sometimes premature conclusions of science, or the ignorant or superstitious beliefs of religion. Books on psychical perceptions as well as the research of parapsychology seemed to offer little pieces of the puzzle. But somehow they didn't offer the real answers that I was seeking.

It seemed that if I was to really understand the nature of these psychical perceptions, it would be through exploring the experience itself, not just the theories. I began to study trance techniques, ritual, and occultism. I never really accepted the whole of these ideas, but I felt that I should explore any possible truth at the core level. Some within mainstream science seemed to dismiss these experiences, no matter how life-changing and fundamental the questions they posed. The diary I had been keeping since my first out-of-body experience was now full, but it was not as detailed as it could have been and I felt it was time to include more detail and go deeper into the qualities and impressions that would arise. This was an extremely important decision; the more I recorded and considered the elements of the experiences the more I was able to develop and explore further. As I have mentioned memory has its limitations, so keeping a record allowed me to go back and cross-reference the experiences for clues to better understand them. I would notice themes and elements that would begin to appear on more than one occasion. The experience with the green sphere, for example, began with a blue energy that seemed to pervade the room; this could be easily forgotten when your mind is focused on something as unusual as a green sphere radiating in front of you. But this blue light was the first mention in my diaries of a quality that I would later identify as the blue or cerulean phase.

4

Cerulean Blue

I had spent most of the last few days at home taking some time
to think away from the pressures of everyday life. I was acutely
mentally alert, like my emotions were fuelling a fire deep in the
core of my mind. I had a lucidity that felt strange, almost foreign.
But for all of this inner energy and insight I felt exhausted,
virtually incapacitated.

I stretched out on my bed hoping to feel better with some
sleep. But instead my mind flowed with energy and awareness
that I seemed unable to block out. The flow and intensity of this
energy was extremely strong and I soon found myself feeling
lightened, like invisible restraints had been peeled away. I found
myself out of my body drifting slowly into Bayswater Road not
far from Marble Arch and close to the other famous monuments
and parks, the grand symbols of a bygone age in London's
history. I could see the buildings all around, stark and white with
the air of royalty and excess about them. Streetlights lined the

large road casting shadows and silhouetting the cars as I watched them move slowly past the majestic trees that edge Hyde Park.

Although by this time I had experienced being in the out-of-body state many times, somehow this was different. My sight felt clear and more precise even than my physical vision. It was tinged with a crystalline tint of cerulean blue, a subtle yet luminous shade like the first blue of the sky at dawn or the distant bluish haze high up in the mountain tops where the atmosphere is thin and ethereal. It felt like I was seeing with my whole mind, like there was a pure radiant awareness flowing through my consciousness and illuminating my senses. It was like looking into a microscope for the first time and seeing a familiar object anew, being able to see the subtle details that are normally hidden from our limited perception. The macro and microcosm somehow unified in my perception of simple yet profound details.

As I continued on, I suddenly began to descend lower in the sky. I was no longer above the buildings looking down; now I was at window height and able to see into the rooms of the buildings as I passed. Small momentary snapshots of people going about their business, and of rooms filled with exuberant decoration. Moving slowly forward horizontally to the buildings I watched the bustling tourists from the many local hotels streaming across the road up ahead as I came upon the busy junction with Queensway. This marked a transition point from the busy populated areas of the West End with its pubs, nightclubs and attractions to the more residential Notting Hill as well as its neighbouring poorer areas of Westbourne and Ladbroke Grove.

It was to be Ladbroke Grove and the area near to Portobello Market that drew my attention; I began to turn in a subtle curve taking in the calmer ambience of the picturesque houses that were still grand and affluent, but that now somehow held a more liberal air. Through the dim streetlight I could make out a white sign on the corner of one of the buildings; it read 'W11', which I immediately recognised as a London area code. As I passed the sign I found myself heading for a road just off of where the market runs. I focused in on a window up ahead; I don't really recall deciding to enter the building, but I turned to the window and effortlessly passed through its reflective surface and found myself standing in a kind of office. Just in front of me stood a desk laid out with papers and what seemed like the paraphernalia of a work place. As I looked at the desk the real potential of my vision became apparent; I could read the details on the page and I could see the grain of the paper. It was more than just seeing; I felt like my vision was connecting directly to my self-awareness, wherever that was now located, not filtered through the lenses of my eyes or interpreted by my brain in the normal process that vision is. The place and the things I was seeing didn't really seem to be important; I felt like I was a child again, learning that I could create meaning by making sounds in the form of words or representing the world around me in the form of simple line drawings. This was a learning ground, an experimental time in which I could piece together some understanding of this new perception. Every detail contained a vibrance far greater than its literal structure.

I focused on remembering the details so that I could verify what I had experienced later; just as I did I started to feel myself 'called' back to my body. I felt myself simply phase out, the scene became faint and within moments I calmly opened my eyes and fixed my gaze on the white of the ceiling, I was in the familiar surroundings of my bedroom again. The sensation of the pillow beneath my head had returned and I quickly came to the realisation, I was back where the experience had begun.

I grabbed for my diary so I could write down the details of the journey and the name and address at the location. It wasn't long before I was able to verify what I had seen, the area code and the name at the address as well as the layout. I was literally able to retrace on foot the path I had travelled in the out-of-body state.

It was a personal confirmation of my experience and again demonstrated the objective reality of what was happening. But there was something even more intriguing than the information I was able to glean; there seemed to be something important about the radiant 'cerulean' that permeated my sight during the experience. I would later come to understand that when my out-of-body sight was tinted cerulean I would have access to detailed information and experiences that sometimes even seemed to be outside of the limitations of time.

Seeing into Time

It was a spring evening when the cerulean-sight returned. It was one of the deepest and most intense of all the out-of-body experiences I have undergone.

I had been busy all day and had hardly eaten when I rushed out of my front door and headed for the underground station. I was conscious of time as I had been distracted by reading and planning the meeting I was conducting that evening. When I arrived at the large dark space underneath a railway arch we were meeting in, a few friends were already gathered at the gate leading to the space. I had just had enough time to get something to eat from the local shop to keep me going before we headed in. We pushed open the large wooden door to the space. The smell of damp hung in the air; the building had the atmosphere of an abandoned workhouse. The darkness that met us as we entered only added to the atmosphere. Its walls were crumbling brown brick; my mind filled with images of what might have been here in the past, oversized machines or tangled cables, track and steel from the railway above. Whatever this place's history it had a strong presence and enough space to lose yourself in some dark corner.

I flicked the light switch, which was almost indistinguishable from the dark paint of the wall; all of a sudden the space became visible under the flickering hum of a dim orange light. Everyone else had found a corner of the space and was removing their day-to-day clothing ready to put something on that was more conducive to physical movement, meditation and trance. I changed my own clothes and sat down in the centre of the floor, to discuss how we would proceed. I described the research I had done during the day and my ideas about trance and how to go deeper and to gain greater insight. My many experiences had by now given me an ability to enter an altered state very fluidly and I was actively formulating my own practices and techniques.

We began the process as I had outlined of entering into trance; I started to focus, but unusually, my mind seemed preoccupied. I felt nothing at first and began to think to myself that the conditions were not right, or my energies were not attuned. All at once a fatigue came over me; I felt like I had been pushed to the ground. In the next moment I realised I was no longer in the space but was now in a powerful out-of-body experience. I found myself sliding down the side of a ridge in a heavily forested landscape. Roots and rich jade green leaves twisted and turned around me; there was something almost primordial about this place like I was in some distant time, some unknown part of prehistory. I came to a halt as I reached what appeared to be a clearing at the foot of the ridge. As I did the sensations seemed to come to a climax and I blacked out.

As I slowly regained consciousness, I became increasingly aware of something around me, large forms, people and lights. This was no longer the organic environment I had been in moments before. These were electric lights and concrete buildings. I found myself standing in Soho, London. I could see the pubs, restaurants and bars, the bustle of central London taking place as usual. As I became more aware I realised I was standing on the corner of Moor Street and Old Compton Street. The two streets form a small pointed area that gives a vantage point from which you can see the length of Old Compton Street.

Moor Street is more of an alleyway that connects Cambridge Circus and the main concourse of Old Compton Street.

The light of the scene was a pale cerulean, a quality I instantly recognised. There was a sense of distance on some level, like I was looking down a tunnel. Suddenly there was an explosion. I saw people running; I watched one man in particular as he ran towards the site of the explosion on the opposite side of the road and maybe just over a hundred metres from where I was standing. The explosion and the emotional impact of the event suggested to me that this was a future event. I'm not really sure why I knew that; it was like I was picking it up from some part of my unconscious mind. I felt the experience was far too strong to be a meaningless hallucination. In fact it was probably the strongest experience I'd ever had. If a future event could be witnessed in this way, then this was it. I was totally disassociated from my body. I felt in another reality, encountering something in a way I didn't really believe was possible. The nature of the experience was horrific human suffering and death in the city I was so at home in. This made the impact all the more complex and challenging.

The aftermath was causing confusion and although I felt somewhat disconnected from the scene physically, I felt like I was picking up on the emotional pain saturating the street. I'm not sure if I could have connected any more to the event; it was like to get too close would be difficult or even damaging. I began to be drawn away as the emotional impact came to a peak.

When I found myself back in my body the trance held fast to me. I felt as if I was being oppressed by one of the most powerful forces in my life; I could not move. I felt like I was in some kind of black hole. I was not alone; the energy that we had connected to that evening was holding fast to others in the space as well; it seemed to be flowing from one to the other like some dark consciousness.

I slowly began to become aware of one of the others in the

room who was sitting close by and quietly humming in an almost chant-like fashion; this seemed to be bringing me back from the void that surrounded me. I finally felt the consciousness that had given me this vision leave; it seemed to move to another member of our small group. I felt a release as this happened and I was finally able to stand up and felt almost normal again. I became concerned for the others, who seemed deeply affected. I had a realisation that to make physical contact with the others would help them to also break out of the oppressive energy pervading the space. I walked to each person, touching them one by one lightly as I passed; as I did they seemed to be lightened. As I reached the last person the whole atmosphere changed and the mood lifted.

Once everyone was settled we sat in a circle and I related the bombing I had seen in Soho, and described my conviction that this was an event yet to take place. One of the older members of the group looked across at me, the artificial light giving his face an air of brooding thought. The atmosphere again became quiet and reflective. Everyone had been deeply affected by the intensity of that evening.

The journey home was full of thoughts about what I had seen and what the implications would be if it were true. The one thing that my experience had not revealed to me was 'why'; what motivation would someone have for attacking a popular area of London like Soho? Five days later, I had been planning to be eating at a restaurant in Old Compton Street; I felt tired and slightly uneasy about the idea and decided to cancel. That night I switched on the news to hear that an individual, who was later revealed to be a far-right terrorist, had exploded a nail bomb in a gay pub in Soho. I watched the live coverage for hours, trying to glean everything I could about what had happened; was it as I had seen a matter of days before? When I realised it fitted what I had written in my diary in every detail, I didn't feel happy or triumphant; it left me with even more intricate and difficult questions.

For the next two weeks I felt strange, like I was in a permanent heightened state. Coincidences seemed to happen on an almost daily basis. Time and space seemed to be much more complex than I'd ever imagined.

It is not easy to put into words the essence of what this experience has meant to me, and beyond even that, what it could mean on a wider level. Time and space seem to stand in the most mysterious of territories. On the one hand they seem fixed and immovable, while on the other they seem to make us question the very basis of how we view reality. The further our understanding develops the more experiences like mine seem to enter the realm of possibility. The exact mechanisms by which these abilities function may be elusive to us now, but new understandings are gaining currency each day; questioning where this will all lead is one of the joys of exploring the shadowy area at the edge of human experience. We may never know how or why but there is liberation in the act of exploring these life-affirming events.

Even in writing these words I have questioned the nature of these experiences. Should they be left out altogether and free myself from the complicated, even damaging misunderstandings they could arouse? Each time I went over this question I came to the same conclusion; to maintain the integrity of what I am presenting here there is no way I could not include this information. It may be challenging, unbelievable and even impossible, yet each experience described in this chapter happened and simple mundane explanations have not allowed me to tuck them away in the back pages of a diary and forget they ever happened. My familiarity with the limitations of memory has caused me to question these experiences again and again, yet the shortcomings of memory cannot explain them; the information was written down before the event. Time seems as elusive as ever and the possibilities are open and inspiring.

The ability to perceive a future event through some form of

clairvoyance is one of the oldest abilities man has been believed to possess throughout history, from the famous Oracle located at Delphi in ancient Greece, right through to the countless prophetic dreams and visions reported in modern times across the world. These areas of human experience have not diminished as time has passed; if anything we have simply found newer ways to understand them. In the past the gods may have been seen as the source of this profound information; now we may evoke the ideas of Quantum physics or new age theories of other levels of reality to help explain how perception beyond time could be possible. We live at the precipice of ever deeper understandings of the way our world works, and it is my belief that those reading these words in the future, if they endure, may have a new understanding, but equally some essence of the mystery of the world in which they live will still survive.

My own experiences of this perception through time did not end that night in Soho; in fact my perceptions were to be challenged just as London itself was to again be shaken to its core.

7th July 2005 London Bombings

It was a bright spring day and I had been thinking about my experience with the Soho bombing since waking. The images, sounds and feelings had been drifting in and out of my thoughts.

That afternoon I came down the stairs that led to the dining room; as I entered the room I felt a shift in awareness like I should pay attention or stop what I was doing. I paused and began to concentrate on my surroundings. The room began to fade around me, first the furniture, the table, and then the chairs that stood adjacent to it, next the wood of the cabinets that lined the far wall. Even the white of the walls themselves seemed to intensify as if they were becoming pure energy or some form of radiation was breaking them apart at an atomic level; as the intensity peaked this radiance gradually faded to nothing. The colours and forms dissolved until out of the nothingness a strange subtle blue glow began to envelop me. I had not experienced anything like this since the horrific sights and emotional turmoil of the Soho bombing. Although this intensity and depth of experience was a rare occurrence, I knew that something very important and powerful was about to happen.

Within seconds I was in the air; I felt the familiar sense of knowing that I had felt in the other cerulean experiences, like running on autopilot, like my destination was already known to me in some unconscious part of myself. Unlike the intense physicality of the Soho bombing experience, this time I felt like a ball of heightened consciousness; I had only a subtle sense of a body.

I was moving now towards Liverpool Street Station looking down at the area I knew to be to Moorgate in the City of London. I could see the familiar entrance at street level; I could make out to my right a circular road or path I believed to be Finsbury Circus that connects the way towards Liverpool Street Station. Foreboding and feelings of empathy and compassion welled up inside me; I felt as if tears might overflow at any moment.

As I moved in closer I could almost see a tension in the air; there was a heaviness, a thick almost tangible quality that hung around me like an unresolved malice. I felt myself move through the roof, my vision darkening as I passed through the ceiling into a Circle Line underground tunnel, the black soot and grey of the concrete instantly familiar to me. As my eyes focused on my surroundings I could make out the familiar underground symbol on a nearby wall directly in front of me as if I was standing on a train at the platform edge. In fact I sensed that the train was up ahead and instinctively I moved down into the tunnel towards it.

As I moved along the tube line, the air became thicker the further I travelled. I sensed that the train was in the station up ahead and I paused as I sensed I was near to the back of the train. I did not continue on from this point; I felt I was close enough.

Then with a blinding intensity an explosion sounded up ahead and a wave of emotions ranging from terror and anguish through to suffering and pain seemed to crash into me. It was clear this was another bombing, and again I felt convinced it was yet to take place. I tried to focus on when this would occur; remembering my experience of the Soho bombing, I began to concentrate, hoping for a sense of the date. I found my mind shifting to another place or level of awareness and in a blurry shifting vision I started to make out numbers, first '5' then '05'. It was April, 2004; "It is either next month, the fifth month or some time in 2005", I thought to myself. The numbers disappeared and I focused on my surroundings again.

I hung in the air surrounded by blackness. I could hear nothing now and I could feel myself being drawn away from the scene; something in me did not want to see the pain and suffering. The feelings of pain on an emotional level were enough; in fact they were almost more upsetting than blood and carnage. We can often disconnect from images like seeing war and death on the news and in films, but we can never really disconnect from real emotional suffering that directly affects us in this way.

I calmly opened my eyes. Although a sadness stopped me from really looking at my surroundings I was now occupied with thought, contemplating what I had seen. The mundane world seemed far in the background. The number '05' came back into my thoughts and the same sense of confusion over what to do next I had felt that night on my way home after the Soho experience came over me. Only this time I felt a stronger conviction that this would happen. I remembered that all of the experiences I'd had that were infused with blue light had either happened or turned out to be accurate visions of a real place. Not some of the cerulean experiences, but *all* of them. So now it was a matter of waiting; would it happen in a matter of weeks or was it '2005' that I had seen in the experience?

The following month came, and nothing happened, so now I believed it must be the year '05' and not the month; I felt confident it would be no later than 2005. I had a year of awareness of what was coming, a year of foreboding to contend with. For the next year I avoided the east/west tube lines as much as possible and tried to persuade others to do the same. It was a hard task as I did not wish to appear crazy or to scare people; it was also hard to avoid the Circle Line as my mother was living at Edgware Road in the west, another site that came to be targeted. It was a strange year; every time I went onto a tube my emotions would well up.

As with the Soho experience it was not horrific images that haunted me, but an overwhelming emotional empathy for the victims. When the bombing did take place on July 7th 2005, six people lay dead at Edgware Road Station. Then came the reports on the news; I knew I had seen the first bombing most clearly in my experience, the bombing on the train that had just left Liverpool Street Station. That bombing claimed seven lives. 7/7 was soon declared the worst terrorist attack in London's history. As I heard those words it conjured images in my mind of the mayhem the IRA had unleashed in London in my youth. The image of the telephone box that blew up on the road I took to school; I remember feeling the vibration as the bomb went off a few hundred metres away from my home. I realised my whole life I had been witness to this kind of inhumanity, that London's enemy had a new name, a new guise, but really it held the same anger at its core. I started to consider that London's history had a deeper message hidden within the carnage I had seen in my non-physical journeys.

Cerulean Dawn

These cerulean experiences have challenged me to understand the reason behind why I would be shown or need within some part of myself to see terrorism and suffering in this way. The result has been an expansion, an openness of mind and an understanding of the importance of the 'real', the 'everyday' in spiritual experience. These encounters with the unknown have taught me the importance of the way we live; they have taught me that spirituality, psychic experiences or philosophies are at their most profound, their most engaged and compassionate, when they are not separate from the world in which we live every day.

When I look back at the days, weeks and months after the Soho bombing in 1999, I can see the confusion I felt, the searching for an answer. These experiences drew me closer to understanding suffering and focused my energy on transforming the hate and frustration within myself, a frustration that I could ultimately use towards finding a greater sense of humanity. Both the Soho and July 7th experiences held at their core not metaphysical abilities, but human beings pushed to the point at which they were willing, even impassioned to take the lives of others for what, in some misguided part of themselves, they must have seen as a greater good.

I have witnessed that same frustration and hate on the streets of London my whole life; people willing to harm others, and to condemn. It is a very human anger that lies at the core of so much intolerance, violence and inhumanity. On the streets it can seem like it's always there deep inside, compelling us to lash out, to express the suffering and anguish in our lives with violence. If we live in the degradation and poverty of a city it is only ever a question of who or what to blame; there sometimes seems too much anguish in us to really comprehend using our energies constructively. The divide between abundance and poverty appears too far to traverse. Being at the bottom of society's strata pushes you into a corner in which you have no choice but to take action or be broken. The greater our frustration or limited our options the greater the chance that we will make a negative, even violent choice. The poorer we are the finer the line between desire and need becomes.

Poverty, violence and social inequality are realities within any life, whether we take the road of violence and crime, or whether we choose to vote for a particular political party who may commit heinous acts in our name. The world in which we are born, grow up and ultimately live, shapes us. In my own life I could have walked a very different path, but much of my attitude towards violence and poverty began years before the cerulean experiences under a dirty London motorway, known simply as the Westway.

5

Westway

The street was quiet and deserted but for a few solitary strangers passing periodically in the darkness, their faces illuminated by the artificial glow of the street-lights as they passed. They walked with their eyes rigid in a fixed stare, showing no emotion or weakness, projecting a facade of strength, or even veiled aggression. They seemed to encapsulate the hardened persona of a large city, so often built up as a defence against our fears of the steel and concrete surroundings.

I crossed the street under the huge grey structure of the overhead motorway, taking in the dark ambiance of the night-time city. There has always been a beauty to London at night, like watching a sleeping predator, a powerful uncontrollable creature lying calm and peaceful, submissive to your imaginings. But this beauty is always delicately balanced with the ever-present possibility that this sleeping predator could wake at any moment and violently lash out.

Three figures approached from the shadows at the other side of the street, glancing at each other and across to me. I knew instinctively something was about to happen. I could see it in their movements, in their energy, in their group dynamic. I had been in similar situations many times, but had somehow escaped virtually unscathed. Yet this time I was conscious of how much older they were than me; I knew I would have little chance of defending myself. I tried to walk casually in a new direction, but the grey wall of the motorway, the road, and the fence on the other side were penning me in. They headed for the edge of the wall parallel to me, cutting me off as I tried to pass.

As they came closer the oldest and largest boy asked for money. *"I don't have any"*, I replied and tried to casually walk on. Before I could make a single step I was in a dizzying spin as punches and kicks came from all three of them at once. I was kicked and punched in the stomach and gasped for air as it became hard to breathe; pain and disorientation overcame me and I fell against a fence. Now with the fence preventing me from moving they upped the tempo, punching me in the head over and over. Consciousness became faint and distant; I sensed that in a moment I would pass out. I think I had hardly reacted from pure shock and disbelief; I had not expected such unbridled violence with absolutely no provocation.

In an attempt to get free I focused on the weakest member of the gang and pulled myself lose. I tried to run, but to pick up speed was hard; I had no energy. The oldest boy got hold of me again and punched me hard over the top of my head. I turned myself towards him and pulled myself free again. I sprinted away and they chased; I could feel them grasping at my clothes close behind. Finally, as I got into my stride I felt myself pulling away; I couldn't sense them any longer. I did not look back; I ran and ran along the long road at the edge of the Westway motorway. Up ahead an old man turned into the road and for a single moment broke his fixed stare and gave me a self-conscious glance before rebuilding his hardened expression. His face stuck in my memory, there was something despairing about him, like the city had overpowered him much like the muggers had done to me. I dodged into the street he had come from at the edge of a park, sensing that I was far enough away by this point that they would not have followed.

I sat on the cold ground, my breathing heavy and painful, my head still spinning. Solitary figures continued to pass me, still with that same focused gaze, unwilling to acknowledge me sitting in pain by the road. I sat for a time watching them pass before gathering my resolve. I stood up, shaking my emotions away, tensing my jaw and knotting my brow. I began to walk, my heart hardening to the world, my trust dissolving. Anger and frustration were building a cage from within. After the events of that night, anger seemed the natural choice; to feel anger and fear seemed the way it should be. This was not a considered position; it was a purely emotional response. I was not thinking at all; it was like instinct, empty but powerful and almost irresistible. These feelings were only to gain greater hold when, not long after that night under the Westway motorway, I was to befriend a group of older boys on that very same destructive trajectory as the muggers of that night. They were probably the most violent and troubled teenagers I had come across. Being around them was full of laughter and smiles, but under the surface there was the awareness that they might turn on me at any moment.

One day while we were hanging around a local park, known for its 'glue-sniffers', heroin addicts and alcoholics, the eldest, most violent of the group decided to show off some knives. This was obviously designed to intimidate and show how potentially violent he was. As he tested their sharpness and made mock stabbing motions in front of me, I kept my cool, but alarm bells were ringing in my head. He had a pale drawn appearance even as a teenager, much like someone with a history of drug abuse.

As he gleefully slashed the knives through the air, engrossed in his private world, his expression suddenly changed. An unmarked police car had turned the corner behind me; he had recognised them as police instantly. His focus changed and he tried to look as if he hadn't seen them. He put his arm around me and quickly placed the knives into *my* pocket, in the hope that if we were stopped it would be me who was arrested. We began to walk across the road pretending to be 'old friends'; it must have looked even more suspicious and out of place to the police than if we'd stayed where we were. Within moments two police, one an older man around fifty, the other a younger woman in her thirties, approached us, saying they had witnessed the 'mugging'. I was separated and the female police officer went straight for the pocket the older boy had put the knives into moments earlier. She pulled the knives out and said she'd seen the whole thing.

They kept calling it a mugging, even though that was not the case; they hardly gave me chance to speak before more police arrived including riot vans. By this time a crowd of teenagers was screaming at the police saying that nothing had happened. The older boy and I were put into separate police cars and driven away; I remember watching the angry exchanges as the car sped off. At the entrance to the station I was handed over to two policemen. They looked at me angrily, still not letting me speak. As soon as I was inside the station the two of them started pushing me down the corridor until we reached a quieter staircase where they started being extremely abusive and aggressive towards me, first the younger man then the older man. The older man had a look of hate in his eyes and wanted the younger officer in his twenties to prove something. He egged the young outsider on as he pushed me around and shouted in my face. The older officer made sure I didn't get away, but I tried to get around him, so they both went for me, pushing me down the stairs.

I'm sure there was some kind of moral belief behind the desire of two grown men to act in such a way towards a thirteen-year-old child. I'm sure there was even some kind of logic in the mind of the young policeman who seemed to want so much to prove himself; after all he was already an outsider and probably believed he would not be accepted without acting with such thoughtless aggression. When it came out later that I was the 'victim' in a mugging, the younger man came to apologise for what they had done to me and, I believe, make sure I wouldn't say anything. He looked quite scared, as if the others would cover up such actions towards a 'guilty' child, but he would have a much harder time explaining his actions when it became known I was the 'innocent' one. As he was still exploiting my fear and confusion I accepted his apology; I just wanted to get out of there, and I was still worried about having been found with the knives. The police had seen what happened so would not accept my version of events. They told me that the older boy had a history of violence and petty crime so it was being taken seriously. That was the last thing I wanted to hear; I knew things were not quite as they seemed. I asked if I could drop the charges, but they said they were witnesses so they would be pursuing it further.

I was finally released to my parents and went home. I knew that the boy's friends would think that I had said the things the police had put into their statements and that I would be in a very difficult position.

The next week when I returned to school, I walked down the first floor corridor on my way out of the building; from that position I could see the school exit from above. Sure enough, the boy's brother and a group of other boys were standing waiting to attack me at the gate. I decided to go out through the back way, but found more of them waiting there; I had to climb the outer wall that led to the park where it had all begun to avoid them. They didn't give up easily, and they would be there waiting often after that; the group would change but they were always there led by the boy's brother. I became expert at monitoring the areas around the school for signs of them every time I left. I stopped going to places where I knew they went and stopped seeing some of my friends. It was a difficult and fearful time. When it did finally end I heard that the brother who had been waiting for me every day had been sent to prison for a murder; I don't know if this is what really happened but I knew he was often armed and was very violent, so it wouldn't have been out of character.

My experiences that year helped me to develop my understanding of the frustrations that can lead someone to lash out or perceive the world with mistrust and judgement. Even after the events of that year were totally in the past I didn't go back to the places where I used to spend time. I moved on with my life and left the events of that year behind me. I found new friends and began to spend most of my time either in Central London or Dalston in the East End. It was like a crossroads in my life. Do I walk the path so many around me were, or use the insights I had been given and define my own life? Many of the local police as well as my peers were caught in a cycle of blame and abuse, demonising each other for the wrongs of the past, while the spiritual understandings I had begun to gain offered a very different view of the world. I was still acutely aware of, and influenced by, the extreme nature of the city but I was also experiencing a spiritual understanding through my experiences and this understanding was at the very least liberating me from the limitations that I was faced with. Unfortunately it was many years before the insights of all of my experiences, both profound and painful, came together. It was to be on the deserted street of a small French village that I would begin to see things anew.

From Violence to Non-violence

Souviens-toi, or *remember* in French, is the only word I recall marked at the entrance to Oradour-sur-Glane. As I stepped onto the path and started to walk past the ruined church and the rusted and decaying remnants of the people who once populated this small village, a sense of the ignorance and the violence in my own heart began to come to the fore.

This place was the site of terrible inhumanity by the Waffen-SS in 1942, and since that time has been left untouched as a way for people to remember the cruelty human beings are capable of enacting upon each other. Every car, every mundane object of a person's life, every aspect of the people of that village has been preserved as it was left on that dreadful day.

The SS began with the men of the village; they were wounded and then set on fire. The women and children were locked in the church, before an explosive was detonated. Those still alive were then shot as they tried to escape. Only 5 men escaped; 197 died, as well as 240 women and 205 children who were murdered that day; only one woman survived.

As I walked through the main street of Oradour-sur-Glane I knew that I was full of the hardened distance of my earlier experiences. I had been defined by that instinctual anger and was ultimately ignorant of the suffering here. My lack of awareness was, on some level, insulting to the memory of what had happened, as well as to myself. This place was confronting me with what had been growing inside me on some almost imperceptible level, a callous part of myself that I had hardly realised existed.

I came upon a single child's shoe lying on the stone floor just inside one of the ruined houses, as if cast off in panic, but now still and ghostly. It lay there devoid of colour from years of sun, rain and snow. A simple child's shoe that for all the world seemed to tell the story of this place in its simple details. Like watching a black and white film, its bleached form played out the loss of a child's life in my mind. A child danced, innocent and free, without hate or judgement, swirling in my mind like a dream I could not wake from. In that single moment I saw the tragedy of the loss of a child's life reflected in a piece of discarded debris, a life that could have been any one of us, or even one of our own children.

I began to realise in that moment I could never accept that ignorance within myself. I knew it was that very ignorance that has led to tragedies like Oradour-sur-Glane. I had never hated a race of people or held any type of bigotry in my heart. My life in London had saved me from that, but I realised an ignorance of the suffering and plight of others, a life focused only upon our own world, is a bigotry of denial.

Many years have passed since I visited Oradour-sur-Glane but it has remained in my heart ever since. It inspired an awareness in me that taught me the value of transcending my youthful angers and pains.

The emotional journey from the Westway to that small French village represents for me a journey inward to explore the moments of suffering and fear in my youth in London. Experiences that planted the seeds of a violent philosophy deep in my unconscious, yet in moments of contemplation, like standing in that silent village, I sensed the futility of that attitude. I realised that I had a choice in how I lived my life and it could be free from these burning frustrations and pains. As the years passed I began to be confronted more and more with the philosophy of non-violence as a working, practical approach to life. Be it a Jain priest in India or a documentary on the history of Civil Rights, I knew somewhere in my heart that I would eventually find freedom from the attitudes of my past and I would embrace a new vision of my life. Yet I also knew this may be a difficult journey.

Non-violence as a philosophy is usually associated with Mohandas Gandhi, who put its principles to practical use against English oppression in India, but the philosophy is much older and dates back centuries. In India it is called *Ahimsa,* a word that literally means avoidance of violence. Yet despite this long tradition Gandhi was not just influenced by the traditions of India; he was also inspired by the work of Russian writer Leo Tolstoy and wrote in his autobiography that Tolstoy's book on non-violent resistance, entitled *'The Kingdom of God is within You'*, overwhelmed him. Tolstoy in turn was influenced by the example of George Fox, often considered the founder of the Religious Society of Friends or the Quakers. The Religious Society of Friends was one of the historical peace churches and held a totally pacifist position towards war and violence. In fact it could be argued that one of the Quakers' key roles in modern society is their involvement in anti-war campaigning and activism across the world, as well as offering space for others to meet for the same kinds of purposes.

When I look back at the events in my life that opened this chapter I can see two paths stretching out from that year; one path would have ended in prison or extreme suffering, whilst the other led me towards creativity and happiness. A non-violent view of life is not simply about not using violence to solve a problem; it also encompasses compassion and benevolence. Increasing these factors in life has the effect of also breaking down the hardened resolve that circumstances may have knotted inside you. You learn to let go and trust others more, which results in their opening to this within you. To demonstrate self-respect inwardly and outwardly, that is at the core of non-violence.

Non-violence has empowered people across the world to transform the way they live and interact; Dr. Martin Luther King Jr. in more recent times used the principles to fight for civil rights and in the present day, Marshall Rosenberg has developed a form of communication to be used in war zones, on the street and even within our intimate relationships. Rosenberg's approach, called *Non-Violent Communication*, is focused on understanding the need of the other person, of seeing in them yourself reflected.

He demonstrates that on a spiritual level for us to understand we must first accept our own weaknesses and fallibilities, to realise that violence does exist within all of us at some level, no matter how we have developed ourselves. We can then understand the circumstances that exist in the lives of those we may have previously condemned; only then can we build genuine empathy and start to free ourselves from the desire to judge and attack.

Some of us may fear the idea of letting go of anger and blame in this way; we are told by our media and our political systems that violence is needed and a part of the way the world is. That strength means power and aggression; might makes right, is the mantra of our age. Violent individuals are often figures of fascination within our media-driven world, often given celebrity status. Our fiction makes serial killers almost superhuman or represents them with genius-like qualities, simply acting in accordance with their nature. The truth, however, is less glamorous, most serial killers being alienated, frustrated and with little understanding of the wider world.

I view the fictional serial killer as a projection of our desire for an unlimited empowered self. In the way that the serial killer may be seeking on a deeper level to be wanted and desired, we too are seeking in them a status and power beyond the mundane realities of life. I believe that to begin to let go of these limiting ideas is a fundamental step towards a greater spiritual freedom.

Part of the fascination that crime and figures like serial killers hold for us is that they seem to symbolise freedom on some unconscious level. The killers and violent criminals stand lurking in a part of our unconscious without limitation, unbridled and visceral. Instead of a genuine freedom we desire power. Take the Marquis De Sade who argued for a vision of 'freedom', but a freedom that he viewed as being based upon a lack of restriction or moral framework, as if freedom exists independently of the experiences of others. Sade did not view freedom as cooperative or inner liberation. His view was one of sexuality, immorality and violence having no bounds beyond a kind of elite hierarchy; his philosophy simply expounded a view of life based upon the cruelty and violence of nature.

For me, first reading Sade's words not long after the events described earlier, I saw a reflection of the angry, violent and despairing side of society. In his words I saw the eyes of the muggers under the Westway and the twisted brows of the people living in fear to the point that they had become harsh and desensitised. Freedom in Sade's world is not really about freedom; it is about power, a deep need for status, a need to overcome the frustration and lack of feeling through cycles of stimulation, one after the other. Sade described a taste for violence; he created this stimulation, if only for himself. In our time we don't need philosophies or intricate criticisms of religion, such as in the writings of Sade; we now have a popular education of violence, a popular 'Sadism', portrayed in all forms, reflecting and stimulating our lives.

I remember my own fascination as a child when my mother told me the story of a murder in South London, which was to become the first so-called 'trunk' murder in London history. She would relate the story of a prostitute murdered and then chopped up by her killer, the remains placed in a trunk and dumped in Charing Cross Station near to Trafalgar Square. The murderer was caught and hung, and the evidence including the trunk is preserved in the *'Black Museum'*, or as it is officially known, the Crime Museum in New Scotland Yard. The woman was Minnie Bonati; she was my great aunt.

In July 2003 I was given permission for my mother and me to visit the museum, something my mother had wanted to do for many years. I had never been to New Scotland Yard before and the ominous guards and security added to the iconic power the building represents.

A group of judges and others involved in law enforcement was gathering in the foyer and chatting amongst themselves; my mother and I guessed that they were there for the visit to the museum as they seemed somehow excited and not in the normal frame of mind that might be expected of police officers. The director of the museum soon appeared, a retired policeman with a slightly flamboyant attitude and style about him; he wore a rather garish tie and shirt, which seemed to suggest he was somewhat of a performer, someone who would not be shy about his views. We were soon to find that our impression was correct.

As we all shuffled along the rather clinical hospital-like corridor we came upon the ironically numbered room 101, no doubt numbered in homage to the nightmarish torture room in the classic book *Nineteen Eighty-Four* by George Orwell. But once we entered the room the atmosphere quickly changed. The room was a near exact reconstruction of the Black Museum, as it would have appeared in the later part of the nineteenth century. The scene was littered with weapons and icons of violence, the tools of murderers and the shadowy impressions of their victims; crumbling photographs, discoloured wax death-masks and bloodstains almost black with time, all transformed into museum exhibits.

Our guide proceeded to tell us not to touch anything as these relics had not been cleaned and were still dangerous; he swung a bloodstained samurai sword over his head to illustrate his point. Next he moved to a wall from which hung a selection of hangman's nooses. His tempo changed somewhat here like he had something important to say and he wanted to make sure he had our full attention. After a few minutes of explaining the process of hanging someone he began to expound his pro-capital punishment opinions. The crowd around me rustled at this and it was apparent that many of them agreed with his violent theory of social improvement. He claimed that no one really cared about a few deaths, even of innocents. *"No one cares about people dying in Africa"*, he 'reasoned'. I was amazed that none of his colleagues thought this a horrific statement, or at least no one said anything.

I considered stepping in at this point but I felt it was more important to hear his true views and to gain an insight into this secretive world.

He continued to the newer part of the museum, my mother and I staying to the back of the group, feeling somewhat like outsiders in this environment. He was now standing next to a bath and cooker with a cooking pot standing on it. He lifted a knife from next to it and started to explain how this knife was used by Dennis Nilsen to cut away the flesh from his victims; the morbid showmanship was showing no signs of waning. I was conscious that I did not want to see this kind of approach used with my family history. Thankfully he did not mention the trunk and artefacts from my relative's case and passed them by, showing us the display privately as the group looked around.

I remember standing in the foyer afterwards feeling helpless, feeling that we really do thrive upon the horrors of life. The man standing in judgement in the police station, lusting after the death penalty, through to the young boy on the street willing to harm another boy, no different from himself, for the status he might gain with his peers. But it is in those moments that I remember the change that is possible, the transformation within my own life, and the result I have seen countless times when people open their eyes to new possibilities.

A wider peace within society grows from the choices we make. If we choose to consider the benefit of others when we take an action, the society we build becomes the result of cooperation and support. Selfishness and greed and an unwillingness to consider the results of our actions are what breed suffering. No one of us is perfect in our actions, but awareness leads to change.

The things I have experienced in my life, both through indefinable perceptions as well as the harsh realities of the city, have come together to help me to perceive things with new eyes. I can look back at the violence I experienced and now see a root to that violence, a sense much like looking at a child that had not yet realised the direct implications of his or her actions. I do not believe that people are inherently bad; I believe they are defined by circumstance. It was not until I gained an emotional maturity, which is probably a major part of what we call spirituality, that I could look at my own life and the lives of those around me and see the events that shaped us.

The emotional turmoil in my life after the circumstances of the cerulean experiences has slowly come into a deeper focus that has led me to discover a sense of peace through an engagement with the darkest of my experiences and perceptions. In some sense I believe that if we are to understand ourselves and develop spiritually we must face the pain, inhumanity and oppression in the world. The spiritual dimension of our lives does not function in a vacuum; it is informed and given strength by the things we are *able* to learn from.

Peace can be strengthened by a deeper awareness of the inhumanity in our own hearts and in every corner of the world, like the impact that a small French village had on me, and its lesson in a single word - 'remember'.

6

Venturing Out by Day

Although I have undoubtedly been shaped by the enclosed streets and anonymity of the inner city, I am also at home in the natural landscape. My father brought me up to enjoy camping and travelling throughout the UK in our blue and white Volkswagen van. My mother and father would sleep in the van and I would pitch my old-fashioned A-frame tent just outside. My father had bought the van when money was too scarce to go abroad, as a way for us to have family holidays. It was an amazing time for me. I was so inspired by the adventure and the freedom of the outdoors.

When I began to explore spiritual practice as an adult there was no doubt that nature would be an important part of my practice. I needed solitude and freedom from distractions if I was to progress. The resources of my immediate environment seemed to have run their course. It was amazing really what I had managed to do with such limited space in my bedroom as a teenager. I had a small cupboard full of incense and candles and anything else I deemed necessary at the time. But now as an adult it was time to use the full possibilities of London, the many parks, woods and heath areas, as well as the places that could be easily reached beyond the limits of London by public transport.

Many of my friends shared a love of the outdoors and as soon as I was old enough we would go on trips together both into the British countryside as well as much further afield. I would also do much of my private practice in the company of just the trees and the animals in the open air. I find that as soon as I breathe in the mossy atmosphere of the woods, my mind begins to clear of clutter, and I am able to stretch out with my awareness and reconnect.

I have begun to see the urban environment and the countryside as almost complementary worlds, on the one hand the energy and peace of nature and on the other the vitality and flux of humanity that makes up the city. Living in London really gave me access to the strengths of both worlds. I could walk into the bustle of central London, with its endless groups of tourists and the dark smoky world of the nightclubs and bars. In another moment I could walk out to a place in the city that was quiet and still, and watch the lights flowing like blood cells along the motorways, bridges and winding side-roads. And then of course there were the times when I would go alone to the heath, and find a space in the heart of the city that was still like the eye at the centre of a storm. In those moments on the heath I could explore, play and put into practice the techniques gained from many hours spent immersed in books. One experience on the heath in particular was to cement my relationship to nature and my understanding of the immense possibilities of trance states.

I found a quiet place deep in the wood and began to focus inwardly, to contemplate the essence of all that was around me. I sat silently in the tall grass, engaging and observing, looking out into the darkness of the woods, my eyes widening in the blackness, disturbed only by the sounds of the occasional breeze rustling the trees above me. As time went by I began, as if from nowhere, to see tiny lights spread out like stars in the darkness. The lights seemed to move as if they were alive - as if they had a consciousness of each other's position, a kind of instinctual sense.

In a moment my self-awareness was gone. I was no longer myself; I was functioning purely on instinct. I was moving through the wood aware of the grass, the scent on the air and the positions of other small creatures like *myself*. The sense of a collective awareness became a method of survival. My thoughts were like pure sensory awareness without complication or doubt. My world was in the details now, in the small pieces of the world I could pick up from smell and the sounds that resonated from distant parts of the wood. The night was my playground, my time to explore and search for food and water.

As the changing light of dawn began to appear I dipped cautiously into a hole, down a lattice of tunnels converging on a womb-like central chamber, and entered the nest of other small vole-like mammals. I moved in amongst my family and found a space at the edge, shifting my body; I felt the others shift in turn to give me warmth and security. I closed my tiny eyes, huddled down and went to sleep.

Morning was bright and sunny and we were all conscious of the danger of venturing out by day. I paused nervously at the mouth of the tunnel to our underground home. Moving slowly into the daylight I darted quickly to the cover of some leaves; I paused and tested the air for scent, before darting to the site of some grain. Still acutely aware, I gathered the grain into my mouth, and anxiously headed back to safety, before carefully storing it close to where I slept.

Each night and day passed with that beautiful sense of instinct and purpose; there was a real peace to the simplicity even though the awareness of each other and the sense of danger was ever present.

Before long the time came again that I needed to venture out to find food during daylight. I moved through the woods aware of the others and my own safety. I did not see the bird of prey coming. I just remember the talons closing around me and the light slowly darkening to my eyes. I had lived a whole life it seemed, a life we seldom consider.

I opened my human eyes and looked into the starlit sky; the life I had just experienced was so perfect, and so simple. The infinity of the night sky seemed to symbolise in its immensity, its stillness, the power of my experience. I felt alive with the life I had just lived; I was totally in the moment and at peace as I walked back to where my two friends waited.

My companion that night was my friend James; we would often visit the heath in the years after we met at a meeting in Croydon. I had been invited by chance to come along after I had written to the organiser simply trying to get hold of an out-of-print magazine. He had kept my address and when the London group began had written to me inviting me along. The first meeting had been an introductory event, and a chance to make plans for the first practical meeting. The meeting was held on a wooded hill that overlooked the city. I remember approaching the group that had already gathered in a small clearing; James seemed to stand out to me. I had an immediate sense that we would become good friends.

The meeting began with a short discussion and then a semi-Wiccan ceremony as we all stood in a circle. It was a very simple gathering, but it had a real power to it and left a good impression for the future. The group was designed to be an exploration of many different paths, approaches and ideas about spirituality and self-transformation. Indeed over the years we explored a very broad range of beliefs and practices, which taught me invaluable lessons in understanding the differing ideologies.

As we travelled back to Victoria Station and said our

goodbyes, James and I exchanged email addresses, I glanced at him as if to say, "I will be in touch". Shortly after I received an email simply entitled *'Hello'*. The first line read, "*Graham, Hi! Just dropping you a line to make sure I've got the right email address and that it works. I also have a few things that you may be able to help me with.*" So began an exchange of information related to a whole range of esoteric subjects. I did my best to guide him with the knowledge and insights I had, but I also wanted to draw on our mutual enthusiasm and do some practical work. It was just over two weeks later that we made arrangements to meet at Hampstead Heath for the first time.

He wrote, "*Graham, Thanks for the email. This Thursday would be good to meet up. How about early evening? 6:30 or 7:00 before it gets too dark so we can actually see where we are while walking on the heath. Do you know Hampstead at all? I could meet you at Belsize Park tube station or somewhere else if you wish... I wandered around on the heath yesterday afternoon and found about three places that seemed pretty good.*"

When we did meet we walked down past the Royal Free Hospital where James studied at the time and down towards the entrance to the heath near to the mainline station. It was still fairly light and the warm still air of summer was very pleasant as we walked along the path into the wooded areas. After James had shown me the three clearings he had mentioned in his email we decided where to stop. It was one of the larger areas, but with a row of tall trees running through the middle. It seemed to be the best of the three.

We chatted a little more before I went through some basic exercises to ground and to create a positive protective space. We must have spent a couple of hours there talking and going through exercises. I felt really at ease with him and it felt great to be in an open space full of trees right in the middle of London.

As I sat on the tube home that night I had a powerful feeling I had found someone whom I could trust enough to work with in a serious and engaged way. In the past people had either been too engrossed in their own ideas or not engaged enough to really learn and grow. James had a different approach; he had a maturity and humility which suggested a person who was willing to work. We were also of a similar age, which meant that we had a degree of freedom in terms of time to meet and study. We visited the heath regularly after that night, finding the open space and our growing interest in trance-based approaches perfectly suited to a more natural setting. The fact that we met so frequently also helped our private practice. We would exchange ideas via email as well as during the walk to the various clearings. This would inspire ideas and new avenues of learning; I'd sit at home reading and then make notes to share the next time we met.

But as well as the meetings of the London group and the work with James, on certain nights there was a totally solitary side to my practice. There were times when my conscious awareness seemed to be drawing me to explore a particular new philosophy or practical approach. On one night whilst I was sitting at home reading about the South American tradition of Santeria, a blending of traditional African beliefs with those of Catholicism, I began to feel unusually alert and restless, my mind full with the sense of something that I couldn't pinpoint. I felt I had to be out of the house in the fresh air and somehow near to nature.

I got up, changed and left, not sure where I was going or why. I just began to walk, stretching out with my thoughts, grasping for a sense of destination. In a moment the thought came to me - Hampstead Heath. I didn't know the way to the heath, just the rough area of north London. I'd only ever been there with James, by car or public transport in the past. The walk would be a long one, maybe two hours on foot. Yet this did not phase me, I was full of energy. I slowly made my way up through St. Johns Wood and then into streets and roads I don't recall; finally I came to a residential area I recognised from times I had been here before. I knew that at the end of this road was the entrance to the heath near the overground station. I made my way onto the heath; it was dark and I couldn't make out anything on the ground. I had been reading about finding a natural object as a kind of spiritual marker, and wanted to mark this night, but there was little chance in the blackness of the woods.

What seemed like hours passed as I walked and walked, but I found nothing. I had no sense of why my inspiration to come here had been so strong. I was also lost in a part of the heath I didn't recognise and had no idea how I would find my way back home. I decided to stop and rest under a small tree.

I stared into the branches, still with a heightened sense of everything around me. Every tangled limb and stem seemed bright, like the energies inside them were seeping out into the atmosphere. As I stared deeper the whole tree seemed to flow and sparkle with energy, until a single branch seemed to stand out from the rest, as if it vibrated on a different frequency, like it was somehow unique amongst the outgrowth. I stared at this single branch, which now appeared totally black and opaque, before the realisation came to me that this could be the object I was looking for, the symbol of a spiritual part of myself. I reached out and broke it away; it came away easily in a kind of Y shape and my awareness of my surroundings seemed to return as I focused on it. I began to see things that were just next to me that I had missed before.

This vision in the branches of the tree reminded me of the story of the Norse god Odin's vision of the Runes in the branches of a tree. Odin was the chief God in the ancient Scandinavian religion, and often associated with magic and mystical trances.

I was so amazed by this vision in the tree that I almost didn't notice that hanging in the tree just to my left was a jar that had been fashioned into a lantern. It was bound with thick twine and a candle had been placed inside it. It seemed that I had chanced upon the perfect place to stop, a place that seemed to encapsulate the state of awareness I had found myself in. I decided to take the lantern as another marker of this night. I left some incense at the site as a symbolic gift to the place, a marking of my experience there. As I got up to leave I was again hit with a sense of rising energy. I stopped in my tracks just a few feet from the tree, awestruck by the clear night sky full of stars. My mind became heightened again and the word *Odin* came into my thoughts. As I stood there with this strange name rotating in my mind the sky became illuminated as a bolt of lightning flashed across the sky followed by a shooting star. There was no other lightning or signs of a storm, just a still dark night.

As can be imagined, there was a great beauty and poetry in the events of that night. I walked out into the street, not sure where I was, but in a state of wonderment. What was the meaning of Odin, and why had it come to my mind? Why had I even been drawn to the heath? I began to make the journey home, again drawing upon my intuition to find the way. I was on a street I had never been to before, somewhere near to the Archway side of the heath, I remember thinking.

In the days and weeks that followed I felt like I did the day I decided to look into my out-of-body experiences and set off to that bookshop in central London. I had wanted to know the meaning of the strange perceptions I had been having, and now again I wanted answers. The next clue was to come in another vision. This time while in deep trance a symbol much like a Rune came to mind. I remember sketching it out in my diary and making a note to find a book on the Runes so that I could find out if this symbol existed. I soon discovered that it was not a generally used Rune, although it did resemble the Rune for 'O' usually associated with Odin. I was to find the answer in a book my friend James bought one day on a trip into central London. He felt I should have the book after he bought it, so he gave it to me. When I got home I found the exact Rune symbol in a list of runic characters. It was the symbol of Wōden.

Wōden was the Anglo-Saxon version of Odin and he appears to have been connected with the Wild Hunt in England, which is also associated with thunderstorms and the souls of the dead, or other preternatural entities travelling across the sky.

In the months after that night I spent many hours researching mythology. It seemed to me that on some level I was connecting to a store of information only available to us in states of deep trance in which we have access to our unconscious. Is this store of information the fabled akashic records, a morphic field, or the collective unconscious? I don't know. But what is fascinating is that information like this does seem to come through under many different circumstances. I have heard countless descriptions of people dreaming of information that turned out to be true, or the amazing details that some children are able to relate as if from a previous life. Obviously not everything that people describe is evidence of something psychical in nature, and we must look at anecdotes with a discerning eye. But there is a transformative power in allowing ourselves the space and freedom to let these perceptions come to the fore.

Our minds do appear, on some level, to communicate in a language of symbols. This is evident from the rich vocabulary of ritual and art that exists in every part of the globe. We as human beings have always, and no doubt always will, express our experience through complex images, mythologies and cultural identities. These things, it appears to me, arise from the moments in which we have allowed ourselves the time to explore our unconscious, whether or not we believe that consciousness is bounded by our brains, or whether we have embraced the possibility that some part of us has access to a broader continuum of consciousness.

The more I have personally experienced and researched, the more it seems apparent that there is some way that memory or patterns of thought and images seem to exist outside of our brains. Scientists such as Dean Radin and Rupert Sheldrake theorise that the mind is extended and that the brain might be more like a receiver. Whether this is the case or not, I continue to find in my life a sense that my experiences connect me to something more expansive than myself. Maybe this is a kind of mystically inspired remote viewing, a perception of things at a distance outside of our normal awareness. Maybe it is that there is a part of all of us that remains constant even beyond death, even as our body decomposes and is transformed into new structures and forms of life.

My own spirituality has arisen from an exploration of the boundaries of life and death, consciousness and brain, as well as culture and the individual. Every society weaves its own myths and beliefs about the way things are, and I believe there is great value in the art and poetry that arises from this spiritual vision. But I also see great beauty in the scientific understanding of the world, the simple yet profoundly powerful method that helps us to see things as they truly are. The scientific method is the greatest meditation.

Siddhārtha Gautama, the Buddha, stilled his mind so that he could see things without distortion or turmoil. Many great scientists have done much the same in an attempt to see the world around them free from distortion, to see the truth.

Spirituality for me is partly an appreciation of the inherent value of things, the essential worth of life, and partly the power of understanding the way the world is, which we call science. When our own symbolic understanding of the world comes together with a wider comprehension of how the world works, the result is something uniquely human, profound and life-affirming. When we look at the great philosophers of the ancient world it is easy to see that there was a similar view. Science, the arts and spirituality were intimately linked. Each discipline represented another aspect of the complexities of life. Science, a search for truth; spirituality, an exploration of our meaning and purpose, the arts, an expression of the human condition.

In our time our spiritual vision, although still unique in each culture, is also mixed with a global view. The mass media in all its many forms saturates our waking world. Many of us feel unable to find the spiritual aspect of our lives. We are torn between the worlds of consumerism and the inner symbolic world many of us long to connect with. In our world a spiritual action can look very different to the one we may hold in our minds. Imagine the spiritual power in our media-driven culture of turning off our televisions; imagine for a moment the power that removing that influence from your world could have. When I took that step I found stillness, I found conversation, I found creativity and I freed myself forever from the major influence in my life coercing me into wanting more and more. In my evenings I now feel connected to those classical thinkers who found their inspiration in the arts, spirituality and science. I make my own choices and I learn and feel inspired and free again. Something as simple as making a choice to shift your attention can change who you are.

I now bring together the meditation of the scientific method and a state of mind focused on my inner subjective world. Creating stillness and silence in my life has been a process, and the result is a rich and symbolic language. I now see in the experiences that opened this chapter a depth that has only come through looking away from the ultimately toxic influences around me, and creating an inner haven, tended with a positive life-affirming vision. We cannot create peace by feeding our hearts and minds with images and views that normalise cruelty and suffering, or even images focused on clothes, products, body image and wealth. Competition and greed lead us further from ourselves.

In those moments when I walk silently into a forest or over the rocks at the foot of a mountain, I discover again a world that is so easily forgotten. A world that nurtures my perceptions and liberates me to feel in a way that I seldom experience in the so-called normality of stimulation and simulation.

When we reclaim our awareness and walk the streets and byways with open eyes we shift ourselves into a new way of being. There is no technique to spiritual transformation, there is only a revolution within the life we lead, a tangible move towards liberation. There is a choice to remove the unnecessary, the stuff we have learnt to depend upon, and to embrace the things that awaken something deeper in your life.

I often refer to the personal, subjective perceptions that come through to us when we make that personal choice, our symbolic language. This is not just a language of words and images, but the way we interpret the world, the filter through which our experience is given meaning and purpose. Whatever we come to believe in life, even if we believe that we are nothing more than advanced organic computers, we still live with purpose, with values and with a longing for a deeper understanding. My visions in nature were, and are, a process that allowed me to map my own spiritual territory. This is a symbolic language that I came to call Shahmai, a personal philosophy that somehow speaks of every culture, belief and discovery that has gone before it. The spiritual language of the world moves on, like any other language, and the future of spirituality to me is in our embracing that change. As I have mentioned it seems to me that religions and philosophies need to be reborn into the next generation, to grow and shift as we grow. The beliefs of the past must die out in their old forms so they can be reborn vital and engaged.

7

Shahmai

I felt a sensation like an electric current being passed through my body. My vision became luminous as if my mind was infused by daylight; it was like the energy of life itself enlivening my body and mind. I could pause and watch as my identity became moved in an overflowing of emotion. I could look into the darkest parts of my psyche and instead of fear I would find compassion for myself as well as all that was around me. In each fleeting moment I would open another doorway into my own unknown territory; I could reach out into a universe coloured by the history of humanity. Every part of the world, every colour I'd seen in the streets of India and every moment of silence I'd experienced in the snow-peaked mountains of Europe seemed represented here. Here was a whole new world to explore within the depths of a trance as ancient as the first healer and as modern as the city that surrounded me.

When I returned to normal consciousness and opened my

eyes again I looked across to James, but couldn't communicate how I felt; I had to be alone, to take in what had happened. I walked away looking into the darkness, silent but full of an overwhelming sense of the limitless potential of human consciousness. I felt I had connected with an archetype of some form. It felt like I spent hours peering into the dark clearing that night. I would occasionally look up only to be greeted by the expanse of the sky and the stars suggesting the even greater expanse of space beyond.

Even during the journey home, as I walked down the long escalator towards the underground tunnels, my mind was occupied by thoughts, *"what next; what does this mean?"* So much of my life had been coloured by these strange experiences that in some sense I had no idea what the purpose was, what they all meant.

As the train vibrated and clashed along the track, I wondered if this was it, the beginning of it all starting to come together into something tangible. So many in the spiritual community see meaning in every tiny event, in every dream, vision or insight. But somehow for me it wasn't so simple; everything seemed more like a natural process, more of an evolution than a grand plan. Evolution by its nature improves upon the patterns and structures of the past and somehow that is what I was thinking in that moment. Spirituality is a potential, an awareness, that I believe is our next step as human beings. In the past religion has held our spirituality captive and made war with science and reason, but now in our time spirituality can evolve and grow in new ways if we choose.

I wrote in my diary that night that there were two things that had been happening to me as a result of spending time in nature and allowing my consciousness to expand in new directions. The first was discovering a state of awareness in which I felt all the creative and passionate aspects of my humanity bubbling to the surface. The second was an overwhelming experience of pure compassion. These states became so identifiable that I began to refer to them by name, the first, Shah, and the second, Mai. It was like the spiritual evolutionary process I had been thinking about that night on my journey home was acting through me, through my experiences out in the woods or in the moments I would spend alone contemplating my life. This process was forming into something new; I felt like an explorer uncovering a new civilisation of ideas and teachings. Was this the unique part of myself that is truly free? Or was that still to come?

I remember the first time I went to the meeting of a spiritual circle in the woods many years ago; that night the experiences I would later come to think of as Shahmai were already in motion. I remember the wonder we all felt as animals and birds seemed to react to what we were doing and in fact even the sky opened and streaks of lightning divided the horizon. I stood there fascinated, but with no real idea of what was beginning. Humanity has always seen great significance in the natural world; some have called this ignorance, simply people with no understanding interpreting things they do not know. While this may be the case on a superficial level, these mythologies and stories represent something of the human condition. That night I first experienced something new that would later lead to my visions of what appeared to be future events.

The vision of the figure as a child, the out-of-body experiences, the Shahmai levels of awareness; all of these things were my peak experiences. These peak experiences connect us to the parts of ourselves that in many aspects of our daily lives we are totally unaware of. In a spiritual sense these are the insights that define who we are, that shape the unfolding of our lives and the choices we make along the way.

It's hard to imagine a spiritual life, a person who has truly gained some insight into the joys and hardships of existence who had not followed these moments of heightened insight. For many these changes come when they finally submit to an idea that through fear or egotistical pride they had resisted for years. They give themselves to what they know to be right even though it may be hard or even painful. The result can be an overwhelming sense of emotion; it may even seem negative or too much to handle when it first begins to arise. These, as has been a theme throughout this book, are the initiations, the changes of consciousness that draw you towards a life that can be truly fulfilling or even world changing.

I see Shahmai as representative for me of the early stages of gaining some sense of spiritual maturity. I don't use the term 'mastery' or 'perfection' as I believe that all of us are far from perfect, even the greatest spiritual thinkers in history. I believe we do humanity a disservice to forget that we can all attain some level of spiritual maturity, that every person has a unique value and merit. Spiritual perceptions take many forms, but there are some which in my experience stand out as being consistent across the world and within many differing cultures. One of these is the set of sensations and perceptions often referred to as kundalini awakening. These perceptions seem to have consistency with many of the experiences of people who are not practising a specifically Eastern or Yogic tradition, including my own experiences. It seems to me that an awakening of consciousness to a point at which things appear interconnected or indeed non-dual is apparent in the writings of many thinkers and spiritual practitioners. Many of these kundalini descriptions include details of reaching a point at which our bodies and minds become full of sensation and intense shifts even in the way we move and relate to the world around us.

The first stage of these kinds of perceptions is often a dissolving of old habits and world views. This can be a painful experience characterised by fearful responses, such as a feeling of losing control. The emotions that arise can be very powerful, especially for a beginner. The out-of-body experience, the states characteristic of kundalini and the other deep trances, can be scary and can also potentially bring out emotions within someone that they were unaware of. For this reason, as with most things in life, it is best to begin any exploration of our inner landscape with caution and simple basic practices. It is recommended to identify one area to work with at a time, allowing the unconscious and the emotional aspects of the psyche to get used to what is happening.

It is not uncommon for these early awakening experiences to be linked to a person. This can be very helpful if the person involved is someone the beginner feels comfortable with. When someone is ready to open in this way they are usually drawn to a person with a particular energy or set of skills who is able to act as a catalyst to their journey.

Spiritual transformation or awakening can take many forms, whether it is through a steady process of meditation over years or through a moment of upheaval. For example, everyday people, with no history of anything spiritual, can be propelled into a spiritual world view through an experience of coming close to death. Some even experience a new spiritual reality when near death, which they are able to recall after having been resuscitated. They glimpse a moment of unconditional love so profound that they see a future laid out ahead of them without fear of death or uncertainty. These people are often transformed in a moment. There is no sense of the journey to this new realisation, and sometimes they can even be altered to the point that they take action to change their lives beyond recognition.

These are rare people indeed, people transformed through extreme circumstances. Yet there are many ways to come to a greater awareness beyond this. You may have seen glimpses of these practices and areas of enquiry within my own experiences or you may recognise moments from your own life in the descriptions here. That is because while the symbolic language of our experiences may be different, their essence or core is common to all of humanity. What I now call Shahmai is subjective, but what it represents is not.

Years passed as I continued to explore the nature of my experiences with these strange kundalini-type energies, and each time I opened to their influence I felt barriers in my psyche being washed away. Until finally on one night I was to confront something totally unexpected.

I could see very little as we came upon the secluded clearing in the middle of the woods. It was a small area almost plain in appearance, yet there was a special energy; there was something very peaceful about this place. I had been here before, maybe a year earlier with a similar intention, yet tonight I felt like I was being called back; I had unfinished business.

James lit a large dark red candle and placed it on the damp ground; the candlelight seemed piercingly bright in the intense darkness. As we faced each other the flickering light made silhouettes of our bodies. I stared at the silhouetted form in front of me for many minutes. James seemed to drift from my attention and in my mind's eye the presence of someone else seemed to come to the fore. A moment later the dark figure appeared to step forward, still veiled in shadow for a moment before the light illuminated his face for the first time.

I felt like I was seeing from some deep part of my unconscious the likeness of myself; yet this other me was somehow different as if I was seeing myself in the past. My doppelganger's clothes were military in style and he seemed almost threatening yet his hands were held together in a symbol of prayer or peace. The threat was simply an image, a stereotype that I knew I must look beyond in order to fully understand the experience. There was an overwhelming sense of energy coming from this strangely familiar figure. I had only ever seen the still silent form of my body lying on the bed when I'd been in an out-of-body experience, I'd never seen a double of myself. I began to sense the familiar Mai energy, the awareness of compassion being so vivid and tangible. The whole space began to illuminate with a radiant light, like our thoughts were becoming pure energy. I moved out into the centre of the space; as I did the double now full of light lifted into the air, as if to watch over my actions.

Overwhelmed, I sat on the branch of the tree that had been so important the last time I was here. I closed my eyes and began to sense the life around me. I could hear the birds above me, and the rustling of small creatures in the bushes at my feet. I sat in total silence and in my mind I called out to James; I was so at one I didn't want to speak or interfere with his experience. Within moments he came close by, walking between the bushes on my left. In the darkness, and his own internal focus, he had not seen me and continued on around the tree as if looking for something. As he came close to passing me for the second time, I again recognised the familiar Mai energy; I realised that James was experiencing the same compassionate consciousness I was.

In the next moment the figure approached me. I stepped from the branch I was sitting on and we stood face to face; he gestured as if to say, *"Do not fear"* and reached out, touching my solar plexus. Pushing deep into my body, he drew out a small black sphere of energy. I looked at him, like looking into a mirror, but in that instant my reflected face changed; a focus came across his brow. I again looked at the dark sphere in his hands and watched as it became transformed into vivid light. The image of myself looked up and placed the now transformed energy back into my solar plexus.

Moments later all was still and other than an overwhelming sense of compassion, everything seemed 'normal' again. I walked back to the flickering candle and again stood facing James. I could still sense a intense energy in him and when we finally came to speak, the first thing he said was how vivid and all-pervading the energy had been. I confirmed that I felt the same; that I had the sense that we had become somehow closer as a result of our shared journey.

The next night I had an intense lucid dream of drifting

through a wilderness. It seemed to contain all the earth's most inhospitable environments, from desert to ice and snow. In every thought and gesture after that night the streets and places I would visit seemed alive with symbols, references to the underlying meaning of things.

A symbol need not be visual or even a solid idea, it need only be a reference to something that contains meaning for many, or maybe only one, person. Like a map of experience Shahmai is a symbolic language, my personal way to access places of inspiration and motivation. This is similar to an artist who creates a unique way of making lines and forms, an expression that speaks only of that one person's core experience. These personal marks or motifs of expression are signs of our attempts as human beings to get beyond the influences and limitations of our world. They are another avenue towards our uniqueness, the core of our spirit, the part that is expressed by the human condition, by our almost endless journey to find *ourselves*.

I remember when I first heard the music of Lisa Gerrard, or others who express themselves through sound via a language that arises from their unconscious, the notion of a personal symbolism was highlighted in a new and surprising way. As with the great artists of the past, they evoke a part of themselves that even they do not fully apprehend, yet still they are able to put it into the world for us to be inspired and maybe even changed forever.

This is the place from which my own symbolic expression arises; after many years of exploring my creative core I found that the unconscious part of myself was forming into something new and transformative.

Art also became a central focus in my life as these powerful states of awareness arose. But somehow I didn't just want to create images that would ignite the imagination; I wanted to give people an experience, something that would possibly even impact them on an emotional or spiritual level. I remember one day in which I sat in my small art studio in North London thinking about how I could create something that would really impact the person coming to experience it. I started to sketch out the beginning of a plan for *Epicene*, the first of what I would come to call my *immersive art*.

Epicene was a large steel structure with a central platform suspended in the centre; this platform allowed a person to lie down comfortably almost as if they were floating above the ground. Once they were there a recording would begin, which guided them on an inner journey. Somehow this seemed the next step in installation art for me; art that was about a creative experience, but one that takes place within the consciousness of the person coming to the exhibition. In a sense this is true of all art, but this took that possibility to another level.

When Epicene was complete I explored many other avenues to having new experiences through art. I explored hypnosis and other ways to change our state of awareness. Many of these explorations I recorded and exhibited in galleries. I was beginning to find ways of taking the inner world and bringing it to the fore, so that others could experience the vast potential of trance states.

When I had my first solo exhibition in New York City in the United States, I was already forming my insights from the Shahmai experiences into something concrete, but I was also still holding back from talking about the more spiritual or metaphysical ideas I held. I didn't want to appear strange or alien and limit my potential within the art world. I now view this as unfortunate, but I was so devoted to the idea of achieving something in my life that it seemed the only way at the time. When I arrived in New York City the curator of the show took me all over the city, introducing me to people and revealing what it had to offer. This was my second time here, but this time I was seeing another side, the one that the locals see. I was also introduced during this trip to Jonas Mekas, one of the founders of avant-garde cinema. As a budding video artist, this was very inspiring. It was all building up to the exhibition a few days later.

The opening night seemed magical; I felt like my ambitions were coming to fruition. I was twenty three at the time and British art was probably at its most popular for years.

Looking out of the window of my subway train as it crossed the Brooklyn bridge into Manhattan, I clutched my Nikon SLR camera, dreaming of where all this might take me. It was a heady time. My nerves hit me as the doors opened and I ascended the steps on my way to Broome Street in Soho where my show was to take place. When I arrived my eyes moved around the space, taking in everyone, trying not to give away my identity as the artist. As the night went on, the people who could see what I was trying to achieve slowly approached me and we talked about the many possibilities of art and consciousness.

It all seemed a long way from the small boy who was so passionate about the work of Da Vinci or Turner, yet somehow this work had the same belief in the human condition and invention that I'd seen in Da Vinci's sketches all those years before.

I left New York with a renewed ambition to make my way in the art world and to achieve great things in my life. Meeting Jonas Mekas had drawn my focus away from installation and for a time I concentrated on video/film work. I was like an alchemist pushing my inventiveness to the limit, envisioning things that had never been done before in any form, let alone the art world. The next project that drew on trance and immersion came a couple of years later; it was called LAM. This time I used computer systems and technology to surround a person with colour and light. I began to explore more and more possibilities. I became fascinated by what could be achieved via virtual reality technology and wrote one of my first applications to become an *artist in residence* at a high-end technology lab. Unfortunately this was not yet the time for me and I didn't get the position. The important thing, however, was that I knew what I wanted to create; I knew I wanted to help take people into the deepest part of themselves via whatever avenues were available.

I began to get recognition for my work, did my first interviews and was offered more shows at locations across the globe. I was extremely single-minded at this time and focused all my energy into developing my work and putting it out into the world. The Shahmai experiences had ignited something in me very different to the out-of-body experiences. Yet both now happened alongside each other and I began to realise that consciousness was a kind of continuum of states. They were not separate, independent ways of understanding the world. They were complementary and helped me to understand my spiritual direction.

While all of this was taking place, I had not been on holiday with my partner Jo, even though we had been together by that point about three years; we had either not had the money or the time to go anywhere. We both needed to experience time for each other and ourselves. We needed to explore our love for each other in a new context and to allow it to take whatever form necessary. It was to become one of the most important journeys of my life.

8

A Revolution of the Spirit

As we walked from the artificially controlled atmosphere of the plane into the rich humid air of Sardinia, my thoughts were focused on relaxing and spending some time celebrating my birthday. My girlfriend, Jo, and I had decided to take the trip on a whim, not even having booked somewhere to stay. Somehow we both felt this was the right thing to do; there was a sense of going with the flow and seeing where we might end up. This was to be the first decision that would shape the way the trip would unfold. We picked up our baggage and got a taxi into town to a place by the sea we'd heard of on the internet. When we arrived they told us they only had space for one night, and looking around we began to realise this was a major destination for Italian holiday-makers. It was going to be difficult to find somewhere to stay within our budget.

We began to look for somewhere else and walked virtually the whole length of the coastal town, carrying everything with us in the burning heat. After hours of looking; tired and disappointed we sat on the beach to work out what would be the best course of action. By this time the sun was setting and I was starting to feel down and foolish for not having been more organised. It seemed that the trip I had planned as a celebration of my birthday was fast becoming a nightmare. As the light faded away, the situation seemed more intense, highlighted by the reality of sitting in the darkness with our belongings spread out around us. Jo seemed OK but I was looking out at the ocean with a real sense of foreboding building inside me. I wasn't really sure why I felt so emotional; after all I'd been in far worse situations, but there was something inexplicable hanging in the air.

We decided we had to get something, even an expensive hotel that was over budget, anything; I didn't want the trip to become focused on a place to stay. After walking back along the coast we finally found a small bed and breakfast, but we could only afford to stay there for one night with the money we had so I knew I needed to find a bank to get more for the rest of the trip.

After a brief break to freshen up we walked into town and I found a small bank tucked away in a side street off the main square and put my card into the cash-point; within seconds it was rejected and my heart dropped. I could not believe what was happening; we had no other source of money. We tried a few other banks in the area but each one rejected my card; I had no others at the time and having not long cleared my student debts I was very low on income. Jo was in a similar situation, and hadn't brought any other cards with her. It was beginning to dawn on me that we might have to make do with the money we had, barely enough for accommodation. We tried to make the most of the hotel that night as we now knew we couldn't stay there for the whole ten days we were away. The next day we asked around and visited a tourist information centre looking for somewhere cheaper. I remember the look on tourist advisor's face, she was obviously concerned and thought we were going to have a really hard time finding somewhere. She suggested we might have to share at a youth hostel. It was far from what we wanted; we said we'd take a look, but after a phone call even that was not an option as it was full. We needed to check out of the room in the hotel very soon and things were not looking up. We began the walk back along the seafront trying to think of a solution when we saw some young tourists who had rucksacks and looked more like travellers than normal tourists, we thought they might be able to help; sure enough they pointed us to some beach-side cabins. They were more like caves with rounded corners, basic beds and a simple cooker. It was very austere looking, but they had space and it was affordable and right on the beach. Having the cooker also meant we could budget our little remaining money for food and anything else we needed. We were so grateful for that strange looking cabin.

After we had paid for the room we laid our money out on the bed to see how much we had left; it worked out to just a pound or two a day for two people. I had come here to celebrate my birthday, so the realisation of having so little money made my heart sink for the second time.

That evening we went to the local supermarket, brought back some basic tinned food and pasta, and made a very simple meal. Somehow even though we had so little, and that meal was less than we would have had at home, something felt right about it. We were in a beautiful environment eating by the sea with the flickering orange glow of a lamp I had improvised from an espresso cup and some burning tissue soaked in oil. All in all we were engaging with the experience; we were making it something rather than expecting the trappings of holiday meals and novelties to give the trip its interest.

Yet just as we were beginning to see the positive side of our circumstances, during the night things again seemed to turn against us. The cabin didn't have anything to stop mosquitoes and as the time came to sleep we realised it was full of them. We were plagued by these biting insects all night, and even had to sleep with the sheets over our heads to avoid them biting our faces. It was a really unpleasant way to spend the night, especially with the temperature being so high. Then as the sun came up the next morning the mosquitoes seemed to disappear, but to replace them large black flies began coming under the door in swarms, buzzing around us and stopping us from relaxing again.

Finally a few hours later the flies had gone and the memory of the night before was fading; Jo went onto the beach to sunbathe and I sat under the palm tree I had been picturing in my mind since London, and started, for the first time, to feel that I could relax. I took out a book on Zen meditation and sat there with the sound of the ocean in the distance and the warmth of the sun gently drawing me into a sleepy peaceful state of contentment. There were to be no home comforts or luxuries, but this trip held a simplicity and humility that were special.

As the days went past we would check our money and make the trip to the local shop working out our budget as we went. I would then sit and read or meditate and generally contemplate my life. It was to become a very important time. I had not intended this trip to be focused on those moments of peaceful reading and meditating, but the trip itself seemed to have other plans. At night we would swim in the ocean under the light of the moon. It seemed larger than normal and full of energy; it was hypnotising as I swam in the ink-black water. This was the first subtle influence that seemed to suggest that something special was taking place.

One day as the heat reached a peak outside the cabin I lay staring into space, glad to get some cool shade away from the burning rays that had little mercy for my fair complexion. As I lay peaceful and at one, after days of meditation and reading, a feeling of peace, light and energy surrounded me. I began to feel myself lifting up, but instead of a visionary or out-of-body experience, I felt myself seem to dissolve and everything I had ever known seemed to shift; it was like the universe had come and entered my heart and that somehow I was totally liberated.

This experience was one that I cannot fully describe; it was like waking up and stretching for the first time. There was no drama or fireworks but everything was different. In that moment of realisation it was like I had travelled back to the night I was beaten by three muggers on a dark night in London; I had travelled to my childhood to the day I was suspended from school as a result of my anger. I travelled within my own pain, my own dark spaces, and had seen the door open, the way out for the first time in many years; I was reclaiming my freedom. I was leaving behind the prison I had built around myself from fear and frustration. I began to sense a shift in values, a realisation of what I was at the deepest level. I felt a connection with something higher than myself, between my life and the life around me; a real desire to make things possible that I had not even imagined before.

When I walked out onto the beach that evening, the moon gleamed above me, its light reflecting on the waves like a shimmering path leading out into the unknown. I felt connected and whole. I didn't know where I was heading, but somehow it didn't matter, I felt enough freedom to not fear the future or the past.

The following year I was invited by an arts curator to work with her and another artist on a large-scale virtual reality art project. The commission was a great opportunity. A few weeks after our first emails I met Roma, the curator, at Foyles Bookshop in London, a place I used to love for their haphazard way of working. The books would never really have much order to them, and you would often find subjects you would never see in a more *conventional* bookshop.

Roma and I went for a coffee and got on from the start; it seemed like this was the opportunity to push my work to the next level I had been waiting for. We talked about our previous projects and how we envisioned this new idea developing. Roma had a real professionalism about her, while her rich Trinidadian accent and friendly air made you feel like you'd known her for years. I felt like she was someone I could trust and learn from.

Not long after we all met at the offices of LIFT, a theatre organisation who were going to be funding the project. They all seemed like really great people and very much behind the project. The first meeting was kind of surreal, I had a bad cold, which should have meant I stayed in bed, but I knew this was an important meeting, so I'd forced myself to go. After everyone had introduced themselves and the atmosphere had relaxed we began work outlining our vision of where the project would go and what we needed to learn. Virtual reality was an exciting new area for all of us and we had to gain a solid understanding of the various forms of technology and equipment needed to make the project happen.

It soon became clear that this was a major undertaking; the vision we had would require all of us to push our resources and expertise to the limit. Over the next year we met regularly and when we weren't meeting we were emailing suppliers and researching new areas and innovations in virtual technology. The project gradually began to take form.

We identified the Science Museum as the location for the project and decided on the physical appearance and structure. We went to visit the building site of the Dana Centre, which was soon to be the new adults only wing of the Science Museum.

Despite all my excitement and inspiration, back at home the strain of working on this project was beginning to show. I had no time to really focus on anything else. My partner Jo was also becoming tired of the project and feeling second to my artistic vision. I was finding it hard to concentrate and felt I needed to escape. Even with my friends I sensed I was on edge and tense in a very uncharacteristic way. In an attempt to make things up to

Jo and to allow me to reconnect we decided to go to India with some money I had in the bank. I booked our flights and within a few weeks we were boarding the plane to north India.

It was such a relief to feel the excitement as we arrived in Delhi; I could see in Jo's face her childlike wonder at the cows lining the roads and the people as they slept in the open air. It was my second trip to India and I knew what to expect, but still I felt alive again, free from the intensity and confusion of a project that, in many ways, had grown out of control. I could sense that my experience on Sardinia had been pushed aside and my spiritual awareness was being diminished in the face of this new artificial world I was struggling to create in the pixels and projected light of virtual reality. The raw energy of India soon cut through that feeling of disconnection. The hot streets, dust and crowds of smiling children struggling to marvel at our strangeness at every corner reminded me of my humanity. There was nothing complex about this experience; it was simply human beings living and filling their life with as much joy as they could. Somehow the power of that simplicity seemed a million miles from the virtual cold computer vision I'd become so dominated by.

I struggled in my interactions with people to remember the compassion and ecstasy I felt in Sardinia, the simple unfettered peace. That spiritual peace seemed to be in the eyes of many of the people we met during our travels. I remember standing in the shadow of a giant Shiva statue in Haridwar at sunrise, looking at a new friend we had made on the train. As she smiled warmly, I could see in that moment where I was going wrong, why I felt like I was walking away from what really mattered. She seemed to have no ideals or complexities other than her faith in humanity. I felt like I was fighting mine. Yet somehow I couldn't express my feelings'; I felt I had to continue to make what I could of what I'd started. Somehow this was not the vision I'd held in my mind that first day when I had felt so completely happy at

Central St. Martins art school. I didn't speak of my doubts and just used my time in India to try to find a direction within what I was doing. We decided to travel up to Nepal and the Himalayas, a place I had always been drawn to. I wanted to see the stillness and power of the mountains, to be aware of their presence and maybe to gain something of their grace.

It's easy to see why the Sadhus, India's wandering ascetics, imbue the mountains with such spiritual meaning. They see the mountains as the place you go to strip everything away, to look deep within yourself in search of the part that is really you, which exists without influence or coercion. I remember my first sight of the snow-covered peaks as we sat on top of a rusty local bus from the Nepalese border. I glanced up into the sky, taking in the white cloud; it took me a few moments to realise that in fact I wasn't looking at cloud at all, but the peaks of the mountains. I'd never seen something so physical, so much a part of the earth reaching so far into the heavens.

Nepal seems to be such a different place from India, somehow the raw energy I'd become accustomed to over the last few weeks was less apparent here. Then again we had come from the intense energy of Varanassi, another sacred place for the devotees of Shiva. But Varanassi was full of death, so much so that the air itself felt dense and heavy, like if you stayed too long it would pull you under like quicksand.

Kathmandu had the feeling of the thin crystalline air of the mountains, the tranquil meditation of the Buddhist monks who enliven the city with their colourful robes, as well as delicate paper kites that the young children fly all across the city. The stillness of the mountains did seem to be at play in the very soul of this place. I knew I wanted to get away from the tourists and main streets and out into the wild, into the untouched expanse of the valleys and foothills. We arranged a guide to take us off the beaten track out to the small villages and then up far away from the modern world.

When we arrived in a small village in the foothills we could see we were far from the normal tourist routes; our guides took us up along a barely visible track covered in loose rock and up into a small village of maybe three or four houses. There was no running water or electricity and as far as you could see, there was nothing but trees and mountains. It was beautiful and within moments of arriving we were greeted by the people who lived there. The children were more wary and seemed suspicious of the strange new arrivals. After some time struggling with a large oil lamp the scene settled and the villagers prepared food for everyone. We communicated through our guides as best we could before pitching our tent and trying to get some sleep. We awoke late, having been exhausted from the miles of walking the day before. When we did step out of our tent the sun was high in the sky and the village was alive with the preparations for the day.

That small village gave me a glimpse of the simplicity I was seeking on that trip. But I was still conscious all along that I would soon have to return to the project and to the question of whether this was even what I wanted to do. Did this project really represent what I was about?

We left Nepal and travelled some more in India before arriving back in Delhi for our final night, which also happened to be Diwali, or the festival of lights. The city was a kaleidoscope of thousands of fireworks, the air thick with smoke and the excitement of children and adults alike. The streets were almost impassable as fireworks were thrown in every direction and people pushed and ran with faces beaming. Our flight was in the early hours of the morning so we could watch the whole event. We watched the last of the excitement begin to dissipate from our hotel roof, while some of the staff played cards. We could see right across the city from there. The clash of spirituality and chaos seemed so symbolic of where I was. Standing watching the explosions and coloured lights across the horizon, London seemed so far away, but this extravaganza was the end of the trip; it was a single moment of abandon all across India before the order and structure re-emerged. I too was about to return to a structured world where ambition and achievement were king.

In the end the project was a success; it was well received by the press and the public alike. Individuals felt a sense of catharsis as they navigated the virtual world alone. They could go where they wanted without fear of harm. This was something that especially women reported; they felt that many of the situations in the virtual world would have been frightening in real life, yet here they felt free, even liberated.

After the project I wanted to regroup, to explore what I had learnt from the process. I began to get back to my spiritual practices and study. I began to realise that on some subtle level the events in Sardinia, and the many years that led up to it, had in fact been acting upon me over the last two years. I remember it was at the autumn equinox that I looked back at a note I had made in Sardinia in my small diary. The note was about bringing together the ideas I had discovered through my experiences. I already knew something had changed, but like many initiatory experiences they needed time to grow, before becoming fully integrated with my identity. The soul and the self often need time to overcome their differences.

As I began to write and engage with my experiences, to travel back into my past in my mind, I could see the ambition, my history in the city and my experiences beyond my body coming together. Like pieces of a puzzle slotting into place; things that had seemed separate for so long now seemed consistent and part of a larger world view. Even things that had been in my life for many years, like an intuitive belief in never drinking alcohol, or my being vegetarian since my teens, now took on a greater significance, as though I was able to see the wider purpose of my choices. These choices meant I was different to my peers in many ways but also somehow strengthened and empowered by the balance of perspective my background and culture gave me.

Waking each morning after the equinox felt different. In the glance of a stranger, or the conversation with a friend, I would see a sense of my changed world view reflected. I had learnt to see others much more as I see myself, to give and to love freely; one of the greatest spiritual truths, but also the most slippery and lofty of peaks to climb. Friends told me that they could see a change in me, a sense of contentment and peace that had not been there in the driven, obsessive part of myself which had dominated in the past.

In the weeks and months that followed, my spiritual direction came flooding back; it was as if the stresses of the last two years were training, a way of making my resolve and ability to see a project through into a reliable and deeply ingrained part of my identity. I knew I wanted to live my philosophy every day so it wasn't long before I started to envision a community or network to bring together people who shared my vision. The Shahmai Network was founded soon after, a focus for the philosophy and ideas that began with an apparition in a tower block in London and came to fruition on a small island many years later. But this was just the beginning.

I remember sitting in my small studio in the basement of my home in Hackney and looking at the drawing I had done some time before that resembled Arabic script. I felt that it represented something of the mystery and wonder I had been experiencing throughout my life. It was to become the symbol for the next stage in my work, the logo of the Shahmai Network. I decided to invite friends to my flat to sell off books in order to raise money for the first meetings of the new Shahami group, a website and also to help with social campaigning. The sale went well and many friends bought books from me to help with the fund raising. Soon after I founded the website and started to research areas of social activism that we could get involved with. By chance I came across the *make poverty history* campaign. At the time I didn't imagine that a small group like ours could be a part of such a major campaign, but in fact that is the nature of such large-scale undertakings. They rely on smaller groups to come together and build into a national and even international mobilisation.

Letter writing, going to demonstrations and getting out onto the streets all helped on a small scale to raise awareness of the millions suffering and dying from poverty. When I would seek to raise awareness of these situations the apathy that many expressed only resulted in my seeing a greater value in communicating these issues. I can't help but think that one day we will look back with shame at the way the rich nations of the world did little to stop the suffering and deaths of those in poorer nations.

From the gap between the ideas and perspectives of modern spiritual philosophies and the situations of extreme inequality in the world, I could see the importance of an approach that brings all of these ideas together. The work I began with the network allows for all of these areas to benefit and nurture each other. As I share my experiences and spiritual ideas with others they can gain insights into psychical and spiritual awareness and they can also become aware of ways that these insights can have a tangible impact in the world.

One of the first steps towards seeing ourselves and society in a new way is to separate ourselves from the influence of society for a period of time. Through silence, solitude and tranquility we can develop greater compassion and connect with the core of ourselves, which can become obscured by the layers built up by the way we live day to day.

9

Solitude and Silence

A retreat is a time of introspection, a time to strip away the influences and coercive aspects of our society. It is a time to go in search of the part of ourselves that exists like a spiritual blueprint at the core of our being. It is in moments away from the support structure of conversation and community that we can start to expose the inner workings of our nature.

The first time I experienced what it is to retire from the complexities of what has become our normal lives, I was sixteen and it was around the time I saw the orb with my friend Gian; in fact he was also to join me on this journey. The trip was to be to the New Forest, an idyllic place filled with the romance of a bygone age; it is the perfect place for a retreat. I had already been preparing for the trip for two weeks with meditation and energy circulation practices, much like the ancient Chinese practice of Qi Gong. I think the events of the last few years leading to this first retreat had given me a sense of focus, even discipline, I'd never experienced in myself before. I could see the changes and experience new possibilities through these simple practices; nothing at school or in popular culture could offer me that.

We left around ten in the morning and although the forest is not far from London it took six hours to get to the cottage we were staying at. We were not disappointed when we did finally arrive; it was a beautiful place, surrounded by a skilfully tended garden, tall trees and an ancient-looking stone wall. The cottage itself had a thatched roof, white stone walls and dark wooden beams that divided the walls at intervals. "It must be hundreds of years old", I thought to myself. I could not have imagined a better place; the atmosphere was calm and peaceful, which was highlighted by the remoteness of the area.

We found the key hidden where the owner had said above the door-frame and pushed open the heavy wooden door into the cottage. The inside was as perfect as the outside; the furniture was old and mostly wooden, the ceilings were low and the rooms small, yet there was enough space to have privacy and solitude. The only thing left to do was to see the garden where I would meditate every morning at sunrise; I pushed open the door at the back of the cottage. The garden was long and plain and not overlooked, which was what I had hoped; the scene was set. I unpacked my things in a small bedroom upstairs; Gian did the same. The room had two single beds and little else; the simplicity appealed to my sense of wanting to have little to distract me.

After unpacking we decided to go for a walk around the small village to acquaint ourselves with our new surroundings. We walked out into the open field at the end of the lane; wild horses roamed everywhere but not a sign of another person. We walked up to the local church, which again was still and deserted. We spent some time letting the beauty and peacefulness flow over us, before returning back for dinner. Part of my practice on this trip was to be a vegetarian diet, something I felt slightly uncomfortable about as my upbringing had been traditional English fare; meat was staple in nearly every meal. Yet somehow on an almost instinctual level I knew being vegetarian was the right thing for me to be doing when trying to sense the subtle ebbs and flows of my inner workings.

As I went to sleep that first night, I had a sense that I was really doing what I was meant to do; I was looking deep into the unknown parts of myself and beyond in an attempt to learn to grow, to evolve as a human being. Part of the reason I was doing this retreat at the time was to gain greater awareness during my unconscious hours. I had been able to enter the out-of-body state and had discovered a world of possibility, yet I had little control or insight into the world of my dreams and unconscious mind. I wanted to experience what is called lucid dreaming, or the ability to be conscious and aware within our dreams, to even control their direction and form. I felt that by totally immersing myself in a state of spiritual focus and breaking my normal sleep patterns I would be able to send a clear message to my unconscious of my intention.

The process as the sun rose was quite simple; I would sit facing the east, still and silent, focused only on accessing my unconscious landscape. In many ways I still see this idea of working with dreams and the unconscious as an excellent foundation for later spiritual development. As time goes by and we continue to work with the boundaries of our consciousness, we slowly refine our awareness, looking directly at each aspect of what makes us who we are - our dreams, our emotions, our fears and our choices. I believe this leads to a state in which we can perceive each aspect of our identity and begin to see the parts that lie at the core, the earliest influences, the emotional frameworks that build up our unconscious motivations and colour our perceptions.

As each day passed I took myself deeper and was able to reach into my unconscious in such a way that my dreams did become more conscious and revealed aspects of myself I was either unaware of or I had forgotten.

It was just a few days into the process when I became aware that I was dreaming; I looked around at my dream landscape with new eyes. The territory was vivid and alive in a way I had never experienced before. The colours were shimmering and full with a depth and quality as though they were the purest colour that it was possible to witness. As I stood there in my own dream world looking at every detail, I remembered the idea of being able to have an out-of-body experience from this dream reality. This was actually the main technique that Dr. Baker for whom I was still working at the time, used to advise people to try. Many books and stories I'd read or heard would say that all that is required to have an OBE is to simply will it to happen or to state your desire in some form. I wanted at the time to master all aspects of the out-of-body state so I willed it to happen. I think I may have even said it out loud, *"I want to leave my body, I want to have an out-of-body experience now!"*. This was somewhat like the affirmation I had used to gain this lucidity; I had been saying to myself, *"I want to be conscious that I am dreaming within my dream tonight"*. Suddenly I was floating out over a beautiful landscape with an intense vividness. It was different to many of my early OBEs, but it was just as powerful.

When I awoke that morning I had gained a new found confidence; I had somewhat doubted my ability to achieve lucidity in dreams, as all previous attempts had failed. Yet now I had not just achieved a lucid dream, but also an OBE launched from a semi-unconscious state.

I continued the daily meditations at sunrise for the rest of the trip, a process I still use when I retreat from the busy world of thoughts and ambitions. I believe that where there is silence there is growth. Silence is a key to spiritual practice. There is virtually no system or tradition of spiritual awakening which does not place great emphasis upon it. Silence allows freedom of mind and possibility. When that freedom is achieved we can begin to 'see' the nature of those things that restrict us. Silence allows us to 'hear' the inner soundless voice that tells us the nature of peace. Solitude is another condition that I see as allowing us a unique opportunity for spiritual awareness.

Solitude and silence are part of a family of conditions essential at least at some point in our life if we want to gain some level of spiritual growth. Solitude allows us to have space to listen, to attune to our true nature. Solitude is one part of a journey to an understanding of humanity, beginning with our own inhumanity and selfishness and ending with an outpouring of life-affirming compassion. Peace transcends location, but without coming to this state of being through times of solitude, progression is stifled and not allowed to flourish.

My own philosophy is based upon a yearly time of solitude. Once or twice a year I undertake a pilgrimage to attune myself for my life in the wider world.

A retreat is the practical application of solitude and silence. Retreats are the spiritual sustenance which allow us to fulfil our spiritual function in the wider world. I believe they are essential to our process of engagement with our inner functions as well as our relationship to others and sacred space. On many levels, until you remove yourself from the wider community for a time to re-attune, you cannot fully learn your relationship to that community. This process often reminds me of fasting. Fasting makes us aware of our body's need for energy and our own cravings as we can see within ourselves the wants and limits that our mind creates when put into such a situation. In a similar process a retreat brings us to an understanding of our dependence upon social structures. It allows us to see the difference between genuine needs and those that are simply the result of the constant bombardment of influences from our mainstream culture.

When I returned to the New Forest, a few years after the events of my first retreat there, I wanted to go alone. I had reached a new stage in my development and felt confident enough now to go by myself. I even felt that I wanted to strip away the need for a conventional shelter. I went with just food, a knife, a blanket and a lighter. It was the height of summer so there was not much to worry about in terms of cold; I would just need to find a suitable spot.

I set off for Waterloo, just across the river Thames in South London, to catch a train to Brockenhurst in the heart of the New Forest. I had only brought a simple bag and had consciously not arranged much about the trip; I felt I should be guided by my intuition. I remember the feeling of focus and peace as I sat on the train watching the rolling English countryside flowing past, fields, wooded hamlets and later the rich colour of the heather and ancient trees that make up the New Forest itself.

I stepped off the train, letting the people pass me and head off in their various directions, I was at a different tempo; I had no need to rush or even any idea of which way I would turn when I left the station; I just wanted to take everything in. I headed out into the street, and somehow my memory of which direction I went is hazy or unimportant; I just continued forward, heading for the densest part of the forest I could find. I wanted to see no one while I was there. I wanted only to hear the wind in the trees, the animals in the grass and the birds in the sky. The rest would be within me.

After walking off the well-trodden paths of the main walking areas I found a remote clearing in the centre of a group of large trees. At the west point of the clearing was a large fallen tree; its roots had ripped the earth in such as way as to leave a rounded ditch that served as a small shelter, with the exposed roots acting as a roof above.

I set to work making a fire almost as soon as I'd arrived. First I gathered wood, then stones to form a circle to contain the fire and some of its heat for cooking. As I sat there listening to the crackle of the fire, spitting as the sap from the some of the wood was too green to burn, I was aware of the almost total silence. The sun was just holding out from disappearing behind the horizon and I knew I was now ready to let the influence of this place take effect on me, much as I had years before.

The cycles of the sun rising and falling from the sky as each day comes and goes remind me of the importance of *time* in a spiritual retreat. There is no way to rush or hurry or even to make an experience more effective. It simply is, and time is as much a part of the process as the other factors. My many experiences on the heath in London, or momentary glimpses of profound trance states, cannot fully realise the power of days, weeks or even months engaged in spiritual practice with no other focus or influences. There is something powerful even in knowing that there is no immediate need to think about what is happening next in our lives, to be able to totally suspend our need for organisation or a schedule.

Over my time in the forest that summer I began to lay the foundations of a regular practice. The act of travelling itself has become a modern avenue to finding ourselves. It is well established that young people will take time out of their studies to travel to an exotic destination, or to live somewhere culturally very distant from their home. There is also the power of the landscape around us. When I ventured away from the locations around London in my retreats I also began to find locations that have a real power to draw people to them. One such location is Avebury. I first visited this magical place while I was doing my first retreat.

Avebury is a couple of hours' journey from London and is the largest megalithic stone circle in Europe and probably the world. I had first visited Avebury at fifteen years old, shortly after my out-of-body experiences began. It became a special place to me very quickly and has drawn me back many times since.

On one visit in the middle of February the temperature was below freezing; the trees were bare and the days very short. We knew it would be challenging to camp at this time of year and exposed as we had decided to camp just a few hundred metres from the stone circle. As it turned out it was to be one of the coldest nights we had experienced. The temperature dropped well below freezing and it quickly became the coldest night of the year.

As we built a fire and began to relax for the evening, I began to cut some vegetables and mix some lentils and herbs to make a thick soup. The soup was warming and we all went to bed feeling happy and fulfilled. Within a few hours, however, I awoke, my breathing chesty and very uncomfortable; my body was shaking with the cold and I desperately scrambled for some extra clothes from my pack. I managed to raise my temperature and quell my shivering but my feet felt as if the blood was beginning to freeze. Around the same moment I heard the subdued call of one of my friends, who had come less prepared than I had.

The rest of the night for all of us would be one of discomfort and little sleep. I decided after several hours to get up and try and warm up by moving. I pulled the cold and wet tent entrance apart and brushed away the ice that had formed during the night. I stepped out into the still dark wood. As I moved back and forth trying to generate some heat in the freezing wind that now beat against me, an orange glow began to push above the horizon behind the end of the wood, which silhouetted the bare winter trees. Slowly as I watched intently the light of a pale yellow sun began to approach along the ground, illuminating the ice crystals that balanced delicately upon the tips of blades of grass. Finally it reached me and my body tingled and overflowed with the warmth of the sun. It was like the embrace of a god; even with such a small amount of heat I felt a sense of its awesome power, the source of life.

A Modern Pilgrimage

I have returned to Avebury many times, finding in its community and landscape a reflection of the ancient peoples and beliefs that once populated the area. These people went to extraordinary lengths to shape their environment in ways that still speak to generations who visit these majestic temples.

There is a freedom in exploring these ancient sites and the landscape that surrounds them. As well as a retreat to a space for calm reflection we can also undertake a kind of modern pilgrimage, a journey to a place that holds significance for many within a particular culture or ideology. Even in a secular world the idea of visiting the birthplace of a famous writer or scientific genius holds a sense of this kind of pilgrimage. It is hard to stand next to the sketches of Leonardo Da Vinci or the notes of Albert Einstein and not hope, at least somewhere deep down, that a spark of their brilliance might be ignited within yourself.

Standing at a site of great significance to a particular world view reinforces the level of commitment we are making in our lives to that particular set of ideas. It is a powerful anchor to travel to a location far away from the everyday world we inhabit. It focuses our attention onto the moment, but also inspires a sense of renewal, a feeling of where you will go from that point to the next. In that context it represents another form of initiatory process.

Travelling holds the key to renewal and inspiration; the new and the unknown open our perceptions, challenge and mould us into new forms. We can't help but see things from a fresh perspective, that of others. Living a nomadic life of travelling and returning, or even one of many new lives, teaches in different ways. A life without travel in some form, without change misses a valuable spiritual potential. Some may only choose to travel within their own country or within the cultural landscape of their community, but growth, change and engagement are the key to learning and seeing the world with new eyes, to holding our perceptions fully open.

When I look at the great art of the world or hear the music of another culture I am transported within my inspiration, I am reminded of people and places that I've forgotten or never knew. Our inspirations are our spiritual food, the things that drive us to grow, change and learn. It is through the tapestry of inspirations that deep connections are formed.

The only danger is in being seduced by the overwhelming nature of the many experiences available to us. It is for this reason that a time within nature, away from outside influences becomes even more important in the life of a traveller. When this balance is reached, between our inner influences, and the lights and sparkle of the many attractions laid out before us, we live with a freedom in body and mind.

The sensory pleasures that unify us, such as music, laughter and love, are the great challenges of this world. Relationships and sexuality form a huge part of most of our lives. For many the search for a partner or partners is the central avenue towards fulfilment and happiness. I believe that sexuality and the many forms of relationships we can choose to explore during our lifetimes is where inspiration and love come together. That is why they can be so important to us. Relationships, be they with friends or lovers, allow us to feel totally alive; they are a way for those who may never explore their spirituality to experience a sense of their core or inner peace.

Love and sexuality are not fixed in my understanding; we can have deep connections both emotionally and sexually with many different people in different ways. This array of possibilities gives rise to an experience of deep love for those in your life. To love and interact with an openness and freedom liberates you on a fundamental level. In many ways the structure around relationships and sex in our culture is defined by a very closed idea of the purpose of relationships. On some levels relationships are about the forming of bonds in order to start a family, but they can also be about exploring the boundaries outside of these limits. We can attempt to discover our own frameworks and ways of relating to others in the same way that we might do when dealing with where we want to live and who we want to befriend. Relationships need not be limited to two people or even to the idea of a partner at all.

This approach to relationships has a lot in common with polyamory, or the idea that you can have more than one meaningful partner at a time in an honest and open way. At its core it represents the fact that love can exist in many shapes and sizes. Gender, sexuality and relationships have been evolving for many years now. I envision a day when these norms will be focused on freedom and equality, not limitation and ideas of ownership or dominance.

For many years it was considered the norm for women to be treated as property and to be controlled and limited, usually through the structures of marriage. The free love movement of the nineteenth century began as a way to free relationships, and ultimately women, from the ideas of church and state, to allow them to take the first steps towards emancipation. Unfortunately in the popular imagination free love is now seen as simply a part of the 1960s hippy movement and it has lost much of its original meaning. Yet in many ways the free love movement laid the groundwork for early feminism and the move towards gay rights and greater equality. It was never about any one idea of how we should love; it was about freedom to define and choose how to express love for yourself. Even celibacy was practised by some members of the early free love movement as this was another valid choice that an individual could make.

I see polyamory, and also its more radical sibling, relationship anarchy, as holding the key to the next step towards a wider-reaching and more profound set of possibilities for human love, regardless of how many partners we may have - none, one or many.

On a spiritual level the understanding that love is not defined by legal definitions or tradition allows us to free ourselves from the need to limit or control another person. In many ways, whether we like it or not, by taking on the structure of marriage we are limiting how our love and the love of our partner can be expressed. This need not be the case and we can learn to understand our interactions without the need for imposed values and expectations. Why for example is the idea of a partner being with someone else so anathema to us? When we consider what they are actually experiencing we realise that this is pleasure and joy. It is nothing to do with our experience, it is about them. When you break this down it is hard to see why so many relationships are torn apart by jealousy and an inability to feel 'compersion', a term which means to experience a kind of empathy for your partner when they are with someone else.

It is not that I am saying that polyamory is for everyone, and most of us will focus on just one partner; it is more that an understanding of relationships based on non-possessiveness is a very powerful idea. What polyamory represents is a form of relating that for many is rooted in a spiritual world view; it is about seeing that love, and for that matter sexuality, need not conform to any particular structure. What is more important is consideration and communication and living in the best way for those involved. A few decades ago the idea of committed gay relationships or people living together outside of marriage was quite alien; now these ways of life are familiar and often celebrated. In the future I imagine that families will take many forms to best meet the needs of children and community and this will look very different from the nuclear family.

Sex and love are often at the core of discussions of spiritual life; for many celibacy is the ideal, as they believe that sexuality can lead us away from inner liberation. Others believe that sexuality can help us towards spiritual liberation, as is seen with many modern Tantra practitioners. This seeming divide is confusing, yet I believe that the reality is quite simple; for me it is a matter of awareness. Spirituality is about becoming aware and gaining a sense of compassion and unity; it seems obvious that sexuality can be a powerful avenue to explore all of these areas. The problems arise when we start to realise the level of sex-negative attitudes that pervade popular culture. People are labelled with offensive names based upon the number of partners they have, the type of pleasures they enjoy or the sex of the person they are attracted to. This attitude is the first challenge; we must liberate ourselves from these kinds of views if they are present to move towards expressing and exploring sexuality in a healthy and transformative way.

In most cases spiritual philosophies never intended sexuality to be viewed in negative ways any more than an understanding of Buddha's law of "*life is suffering*" was meant to make us view all life in a negative way. Sexuality was seen as an area to which we could become attached in a way that draws us away from our awareness. The spiritual teachers of the world have given us a vision of understanding our needs, our emotions and our cravings with conscious awareness. From this understanding sexuality is one of the most important areas for us to explore because it defines so much of our culture. What I envision is a sexuality not of fashion, consumerism or pornography, but a sexuality of exploration, unity and awareness - a sacred sexuality.

As with the retreat from the coercive aspects of society we have already discussed, celibacy is a way of taking time to look deeply at the influences and feelings that define our sexual identity. I do not view this as a permanent ideal, any more than living in the wilderness forever is an ideal. It is a process towards becoming aware, like fasting or meditation. It is a time to step away from our everyday actions to view them with fresh eyes. Anyone who is going to explore their sacred sexuality will benefit from taking the time to experience a time of abstinence.

All of these many aspects of my practice and life form a circle, a loop of philosophy and action. Somehow throughout my life I have always known on an instinctual level that truth exists in many forms; that spiritual truth, or a deep awareness of love or unity, is as valid and important as the scientific truth of knowledge. They complement and enhance each other, so in my life I envision a spiritual philosophy that would put genuine learning, growth and change at the core. I don't just mean this in the journey towards spiritual maturity already discussed; I mean it in the sense that outdated ideas and the things that spiritual people were mistaken about in the wider arena of religion and culture can be allowed to dissolve. Our focus on the sacred words of those we choose to idealise can hold us back from moving forward.

When we consider maturity in any area of life it includes the notion of letting go of the childish or ignorant beliefs of the past; spirituality also needs this letting go process. The religions of the world have often held fast to the ideas of bygone times and forgotten to see the lives and communities of the past in the context that surrounded and defined them. We once believed many things about the universe we now know to be mythology, or visions born from the human mind of how the world might be. There is great beauty in many of these visions, but we now have the collective learning of generations to build our under-standing from.

In my own attempt to outline a spiritual philosophy I have held in the forefront of my mind the belief that these ideas will grow and evolve over time. I also remember the humility of not knowing. When we approach any knowledge I believe it is extremely important to have the humility to say you don't know. There are many ideas about spiritual and psychical reality but the best position is to be aware that we might not be correct in our perception of reality. In fact we should be aware that it is actually highly likely that we are wrong. If we weigh all of the information we are surrounded by every day it becomes obvious that our grasp of all these elements will be limited, no matter who we are. I believe we should learn from this in the way we think about our experiences and the knowledge we come into contact with.

It is a process of refining our world view and using a benevolent attitude as our most fundamental guide. We are all flawed, yet spiritual truth has always tried to focus on love, which is really another way of expressing unity, peace, and an understanding of others. It is ultimately a philosophy of benevolence.

10

A Philosophy of Benevolence

We are never truly individual. We are always a part of a family, a group and a community. When we start to consider our debt to others, the sheer amount of energy we have drawn from the community and from the world, we can begin to see that we are not just on an emotional and intellectual level a part of a group, but also on an internal level. Virtually all of the things that make up our identity are given to us by our cultures, families and heritage. Sharing and interacting are part of how we have become who we are; they are far deeper and more important to our lives than we often imagine. Culture, science, morality and in fact the very way we think and what we think are a result of influence and exchange, the very essence of community.

We might ask at what points in our life are we truly alone? Could it be at birth and at death? These are two points of non-existence that hold within them the seeds of a life to live and a life lived. Maybe we find in those moments the part of ourselves that lies at our core, the part of us beyond words and sociali-sation.

The near death experiences mentioned earlier or the profound states of awareness people experience in various forms of ritual and meditation tend to draw us to a point at which we can feel connected to everything and everyone. These states help us to become aware of the non-separate nature of our existence. The moral and social ideas of compassion, non-violence and even love come from an awareness of oneness with at least one other, a sense that we have transcended separation, that to harm another would be like harming ourselves. Even the language we use when talking of love, the idea of finding 'our other half' implies that through our relationships we find wholeness.

All morality, at least in part, draws from some sense of trying to understand the experience of another person, trying to avoid the suffering or pain of someone else by structuring the way we live towards an avenue of the least harm. The *Golden Rule* or the *Ethic of Reciprocity* is one of the oldest principles that draws upon the idea of understanding the suffering of others as ourselves. The earliest version of it dates back to ancient Egypt from *The Tale of the Eloquent Peasant*. It reads *"Do for one who may do for you, that you may cause him thus to do"*. This simple principle of treating others as yourself has endured to this day and for many is the most valuable of all moral guides.

Another idea that underlines and complements the Golden Rule is, *we fear that which we do not understand.* We act contrary to the Golden Rule because we do not understand others; we do not see in them our failings reflected back, we do not perceive the inherent unity of all life. So this idea holds within it the key to creating harmony, to understanding the beliefs, and more impor-tantly, the actions, of others. There are always limits to this idea and we must remember that the abuse committed by someone else is never our fault or responsibility. But in the more everyday situations in which we judge and create division these core ideas of seeing ourselves in others can help us to understand others in a new way, that brings us together.

I think in many ways these simple ideas are what religions across the world try to communicate, but often get too entwined in their particular world view to see the value in other views and ways of life. It is a real strength of modern understandings of spirituality that they can step outside of these rigid forms of viewing the world and use the simple principle of not having all the answers as a strength, not a weakness or shortcoming. To fill our minds with things that have no real meaning simply to have a world view is not a strength.

For me religions have sought to explain and give meaning to the world, which has given us great cultural and artistic traditions and defined much of our humanity. However, the idea that these simple mythologies can explain things such as the origin of life or the ultimate nature of reality is flawed. We do not need religion for meaning. Meaning is derived from understanding, not simply from the reality or not of a higher being or other supernatural reality. In my view as we progress and develop as a species we learn more about ourselves and our universe and through that we gain greater insight and meaning, not less. Whether something is made or arises by chance is not the sum of its worth. We are in this world whether created or by the natural process of evolution or not. The power is in our ability as conscious beings to choose a benevolent and peaceful life.

My vision is of a spirituality rooted in a scientific method of viewing the world as it is, while also embracing the power of human potential; envisioning a community of cooperation and compassion.

There are many ideas that draw upon both secular and spiritual understandings of the world. One moral understanding that is very close to my heart is the issue of other species and our use of them. Philosophers such as Peter Singer, author of *Animal Liberation*, come at their views from a purely secular system of reasoning, while religious and spiritual frameworks such as Jainism also puts across the notion of the value of other species. The tenets of Jainism state *"Just I dislike pain, so all other beings dislike pain"*, and *"Respect for all living beings is non-violence; non-violence is the highest religion."* It is easy to see reflected in these statements the Golden Rule and other moral notions already discussed. These philosophies, whether secular, spiritual or somewhere in between all express that

the worth of life is not its worth to us. I believe that a person or society who does not stand against the view that the value of other species is based purely upon the level of their use to us, or their intelligence, is doomed to slavery. For such an apathetic society will likely not stand against the inhumanities enacted upon the weak or poor by their own representatives.

I think this is what many have been getting at in their writings, the belief that we must stand up for the weakest within our societies, to paraphrase Gandhi. Even Leonardo Da Vinci and Leo Tolstoy echoed this notion, believing that while we see animals as mere products for our use, wars and inhumanity will always exist within our own species.

My thoughts on the use of other species began many years ago. As a young man my father worked at Smithfield market, one of the most historic markets in London, renowned for its meat from all over the world. In fact there has been a market at the site for nearly a thousand years. Not surprisingly meat was a staple of my diet throughout my early childhood. I have many memories of my father skilfully reducing a carcass to various parts or 'cuts' for cooking and storage. Ironically I never really liked meat and would often struggle to eat it, especially the fleshy fat that would make me heave. Maybe I was too conscious of what it was I was eating; other children were simply unaware or could ignore or forget the details, having only ever seen meat in plastic packets presented in much the same way as any other 'product'. Most people do seem able to view meat simply as a product but occasionally the realities become apparent, even within the industry itself. My father once related the story of a farmer who had become close to his prize bull, but finally brought the huge animal to the slaughter house that used to stand in Caledonian Road. He couldn't watch the death of this powerful old bull he had grown so close to. Instead he spoke to the men and asked them to kill it with as little pain as possible. This of course is far from easy when faced with such a large animal. And really it's likely he knew the reality would be very different. They decided to poleaxe it to death, a process that involves caving in the head of the animal with an object that looks something between a sledgehammer and an axe. The bull resisted and used its weight and strength to pull away from the men. It took many workers and several attempts to bring him down and finally strike the blow that killed him.

Since those days we have focused on the welfare of animals to ease our conscience about the needless killing. We have built up an image of an animal having a life and then being killed without pain. Yet this is far from the truth. Even if the death itself is painless, a cow, for example, is killed after a year or two maximum; a fraction of the 30 or more years it would naturally live. No matter how we try to avoid it, animals are seen simply as things, as objects for our use; their lives and happiness matter less to us than the taste of their flesh. No wonder we live in a world dominated by ruthless self-interest.

We live in a world of mechanised farming where the life of animals is reduced to a product on a production line. We fool ourselves into believing that there is such a thing as humane meat, that humane killing exists. Animals suffer at every level of the process, but this is only part of the issue. Many of us now look around and see the destruction that human beings are doing to the world as a result of our belief that we are its rulers. We look to greener fuels and ways of producing energy, yet the animals we exploit and kill are overlooked. On a simple environmental level, meat production wastes precious resources, such as plant protein and water, and according to some produces more CO_2 than all cars and planes put together. These situations come from the disconnection we make from the reality of how we treat the world around us. My understanding is one of living within the world, not off the world. Respect is an understanding of the inherent value of all things. From a spiritual and ethical position, we must respect all life and the subtle harmony of the world around us.

When I think back to myself as a child, not being able to get the repulsive idea of what it was I was eating out of my head, I see that that was the beginning of my being able to make the connection between my actions and the world outside. I went through a long process of trying to maintain the disconnection, but ultimately the seed of change was already growing.

It was health and a belief that vegetarianism was somehow more spiritual, although I had no real idea why, that led me to first explore living without meat. But the real change came when I began to work directly on myself in a spiritual context, the aftermath of my transformative experience in Sardinia. I felt connected to other life; I became increasingly aware of the similarity of other forms of life to us, that they too experience happiness, feel pain, and even loss. I also realised that I was living a life that financed death and suffering, as well as environmental damage and harming myself at the same time. All of these factors seemed to underline how wasteful and unnecessary meat and dairy are in our lives.

I hesitantly began to explore the realities of our use of non-human animals, and it became clearer and clearer that I would have to change in ways that, at the time, I feared. The word 'vegan' for example conjured up negative images in my mind. Yet as I learnt more I found that even great athletes such as Carl Lewis, the American track and field athlete who won ten Olympic medals including nine golds, and is arguably one of the greatest athletes of all time, was vegan when he achieved his greatest performances. This didn't fit my image, and as a track athlete myself in my early teens, I had a lot of respect for Lewis's performances. The more I looked the more the negative image I held was destroyed by the truth, the reality of veganism in the world. I could see there were health benefits, ethical and environmental benefits; in fact on every level it was the only way a compassionate, healthy, and engaged person could live once they were aware of the issues.

I think an awareness of the issues of speciesism, the belief that humans have the right to use animals in any way we see fit, was what led Dexter Scott King and then his mother Corretta Scott King, the wife of Martin Luther King Jr, to both become vegan. Dexter Scott King could, no doubt, see that his father's legacy of non-violent change and a belief in the notion that might does not make right, is easily extended to the voiceless within our world - other species.

Many of our ideas about exploiting anything or anyone are rooted in how we view those individuals; women for example were seen as intellectually inferior to men and therefore men felt justified in oppressing them. I see many parallels in the history of humanity to the current struggle for animal liberation.

The level of awareness or intelligence an animal is capable of is another justification used for our abusive actions. We need to ask ourselves, is the worth of a life decided by intellect alone? Or maybe the worth of a life is decided by the ease with which that life may be exploited?

Once people of African descent were seen as objects for exploitation, or 'chattels' as the slave traders called them; it was accepted because one group had the resources to dominate another. The slave traders had more technology and trading resources so they exploited the weaknesses of other nations or peoples. We now look back at this time with shame, because the ancestors of modern Americans and Europeans failed to act with humility and equality. Non-human animals are not equal in intellect and are easily dominated, so the suffering of certain of their kind is widely accepted.

Many will resort to nature as a justification of their lifestyle at this point. A view of nature as a singular system of domination of one over another, or many, has been used throughout modern history to justify bigotry and intolerance. This view of nature is of an almost static force, an environment based upon a simple overriding principle, 'survival of the fittest'. This phrase is often attributed to Charles Darwin's On the Origin of Species, but in fact was coined by Herbert Spencer in 1864 shortly after the publication of Darwin's work. Furthermore 'fittest' at that time meant 'most suitable' not the 'strongest' or most able to dominate or overcome. In fact Darwin and most modern scientists use the term 'natural selection'. In the light of natural selection nature can be viewed as multi-layered, which reveals how diversity is as much a part of the natural world as it is a part of human behaviour.

The nature argument in virtually all its forms is simply a convenient justification for conformity, rather than change and development. Nature has always been diverse and complex, far from simplistic opposites and full of unusual and surprising behaviours. All of humanity use methods or practices that are unique and more developed than the animal kingdom; thus arguments of humans justifying their action based on what is natural are inherently flawed. In fact in many circles the appeal to nature is seen as a logical fallacy, much like the appeal to authority or status. In my view these nature arguments represent the last resort in a limited world view that attempts to step away from the idea of a better human condition in which the rights and lives of all are respected and nurtured as humanity's greatest moral understandings.

When I think back to the dominance and violence that underlined my experiences at the Westway, I can see that my views and understandings have grown out of a shift in my own personal perspective on peace and freedom. As I have learnt and developed I have gained a sense of peace as a state that liberates us from the need for justifications of why we act in certain negative ways, such as those of a violent nature, or that history or tradition makes negative and destructive actions acceptable.

However, we must also remember that we cannot judge the use of violence; it is a part of us all, and in the right circumstances it will come to the fore. The defence of a loved one or someone weaker than ourselves is often the line that will lead to violence in many generally peaceful people. I believe the key is that we realise this and start to actively alleviate the roots of violence, the avenues that lead to a situation so extreme that the most peaceful person will see little choice but to act. Those roots are the stress, isolation and frustration that lead to anger and violence across our societies. In a practical sense we must look at poverty, inequality and the things that we accept in our lives, the images, words and attitudes. We must seek to express another way, an empowering way that does not perpetuate violent feelings. As we make changes around us we create a peaceful society and as I have said the margins and possibilities for violence are lessened.

Some even fear ideas like peace, as if a state free of anger or violence were a weakness. For me that is to embrace the very nature of violence, the fear that underlines and permeates violent acts. Non-violence and peace exist in the context of the community, the non-individualistic awareness that I began this chapter describing. They are about how we act in the world, how we react and go through our interactions with others. They are the realisation that we have choices in how we relate and how we perceive the actions of others. This is a very powerful awareness, like seeing ourselves in others; we can also find a sense of deep empathy and fulfilment by opening our actions, by seeing others as kindred spirits searching for love and freedom in the same way as us.

Living with an openness of this type is more than just a peaceful life; it is a fearless life. It is a statement to ourselves and others that we will not fear. We will not walk the streets thinking of the violence of others or seeing in the faces of strangers anything other than a human being searching for the same things as us. Whether spiritual master, murderer or genius, I see in them the same humanity, the same failings, vulnerabilities and short-comings we all possess. There is no perfection, only those who have learnt to understand the nature of their imperfections.

Many see spiritual perfection as a kind of infallible state, a centred space that is not challenged or defeated by any condition in life. It is the strength that overcomes all pain and adversity. It is a state free of fear, and therefore free of violence. The classic illustration of this view of perfection is the image of a man being put to death, but still he knows no hatred; he is truly free.

The concept of perfection above speaks of the pinnacle of inner liberation, an inner peace that is so all-encompassing that it renders the person incapable of harm or malice. Yet I am drawn to view this kind of inner tranquillity not as a condition or state at all; it is the avenue to overcoming the things that would undermine harmony, such as violence, oppression and intol-erance. Take the story of Jesus Christ; he spoke in the Sermon on the Mount of turning the other cheek and not reacting to violence. Yet he is also seen in a rage when he finds gambling taking place in the temple. It is not that people who understand peace are incapable of reaction or emotional outpouring; more that when they are faced with the darkest elements of the human experience they are able to evoke a power to make their own choice, to not be influenced to violence, to not be overcome by the coercion of society or their own emotions. Again they have learnt to understand their own fallibilities.

I once got depressed because I was unable to control my temper during a serious argument. Then a friend said, "Why? Did *you expect to have overcome anger? Did you expect to get to a point where it was simply impossible?"* It was true; our emotions are a part of us that we must be aware of and work with on an ongoing basis. We do not arrive at an unchanging state - we learn to live with an 'awareness' of who and what we are from which we can cultivate peace. Peace is not a place or an end point; it is a part of us that we must cultivate and nurture beyond our normal cycles and limitations.

A sense of peacefulness free of all emotion is not a desirable condition for most of us. Most of humanity wish to experience the full spectrum of emotion, something that gives us our humanity, that makes us feel and love. We see in great musicians, artists and thinkers that passion and sometimes emotional turmoil can help these creative people to access the deepest resources within themselves. Many of us have this lingering in our minds when we explore what it is to be spiritual and are often torn by an illusory division between what we may see as polar opposites. I believe that it is a mistake to see these emotional and spiritual aspects of life as opposite; they are both on the spectrum of spiritual understanding and should be embraced as such. True spirituality is simply about freedom, compassion and growing awareness. Anything that can draw you towards these things can be a part of the spiritual journey.

In many ways it is when the inner awareness of spirituality comes together with a powerful sense of emotion, empathy and a sense of justice, that great social change is born. Mohandas Gandhi's anger at being thrown from a train in South Africa led to the independence of India from English rule. This was not simply the result of the spiritual approaches that Gandhi employed later; it was also his humanity, his frustration and feeling of injustice that fired his drive for change.

I feel that change within society grows from the choices we make, but also from the empathy we have gained. If we have a deeper understanding of others when we take an action, the society we build and the community we see develop becomes the result of cooperation and support. Selfishness and greed and an unwillingness to consider the results of our actions are what breed contempt. People can become blinded to their own attitudes because they have simply taken on the attitudes of society, many of which are simply some form of consumerism. The world of consumerism seduces us with products, with objects of desire that have a consequence. Every item we buy in an unjust or unethical society moves us away from an equal world and positive society.

Governments fill us with fear and normalise war and inequality. I believe that war and many of the inequalities around us originate out of a distorted view of what we need, of what is important. It seems that extreme actions such as wars arise out of a misunderstanding of the nature of peace. This misunderstanding takes hold when peace becomes replaced or synonymous with security. We start to mistrust and believe that we must protect ourselves from some threat or other when often there is little or none.

Fear is the basis upon which we look to security for the answer, for the way to sustain a peaceful society. It is a similar fear-driven belief, which makes war to bring about peace, or puts up walls and bars to make a society and community better. These fears are not part of a truly peaceful way of life; true peace is dependent upon an absence of irrational fear. This is where the relationship between our inner and outer worlds comes to the fore. Creating a balance between the symbols of fear internally and externally is one step towards greater happiness. We must seek to liberate ourselves from the symbols of fear; weapons for one are something we can remove easily from our lives.

I once met a peaceful man who felt that money was at the core of his fear and that of those around him, so he had for many years denounced its use. Imagine for a moment the power inherent in such an action. We live in a society dominated by the desire for personal wealth for no other purpose but our own selfish pleasure, ignorantly oblivious to the suffering of millions. Imagine for a moment the power of using money for good, of denouncing the use of money for greed.

Such changes in belief can lead to the simplifying of life and the nurturing of compassion. There are many avenues to life changing choices, the more we look at the fear within us and our societies the more these choices become liberating acts towards greater peace and awareness.

Recently within my own life I have undergone major changes in how I experience fear and how I approach my needs. A long relationship had ended and new possibilities had been opening to me since then. All this was building up to a desire to explore where the next few years would lead. My spirituality had been gradually evolving over the last decade and now I was in a position to go in any direction without limitation. At the time I was still living by the sea, something I really enjoyed. I could walk down to the water's edge and just listen, sit and meditate in the presence of the vastness of the horizon, waves and sky above. I would often just walk, taking in the beauty of the clouds in shades of purple, orange and pink.

Being in this environment by the sea helped me to heal and to get ready to move forward in my life. I suppose I had failed in some ways to be truthful during my relationship and now I was beginning to get the drive to be totally honest about my desires and needs. I was not going to fear revealing myself in future relationships.

I would often do something that was not really what I wanted out of fear of the consequences of being true to myself. Many of us do this, especially in relationships. Yet somehow when we identify what our true needs and desires are and we learn to be open about them, even when we fear we will be judged, the result is that we push away those who don't nurture and respect us, but we also attract those who do. This level of truthfulness liberates us to be ourselves in the most basic interactions with others right through to the deepest levels of our spiritual core. It results in an inner peace and calm that only comes from a genuine sense of freedom. Being true to what is most integral to ourselves without fear of judgement is the real emancipation of the soul.

My out-of-body experiences also began to reflect my expanding sense of core honesty. Looking back now it doesn't surprise me that it would be my OBEs that revealed this to me; I have been shown so much through these enigmatic experiences throughout my life.

It was actually around the anniversary of my first intentional experience. Waves of energy began running through my body and a sense of my legs and arms lifting up away from my torso. As I left my body I couldn't make anything out in the blackness, just a sensation of movement. After a time I felt as if I had come to a stop and I began to focus on opening what seemed to be my eyes. As I did they were met by a deep translucent blue, edged by the purest black I have ever seen. The colours mesmerised me with their brilliance and for a moment I thought I had returned to the ethereal levels that seem to lie outside of this reality. Yet instead I began to recognise the gradual formation of what I realised was the Earth's atmosphere like a wall of mist in the sunlight. I could sense the subtle, almost indiscernible rotation of the planet as I hung in the air at the threshold of the vast expanse of space, the curvature of the Earth disappearing into the distance.

I watched the shapes and swirls of oceans and continents far below, unable to apprehend their full beauty. In the tranquillity of that moment I considered the future; I wondered what will happen to this beautiful planet and the abundant life that exists on its surface. I wondered what choices we will make as a species and whether we will liberate ourselves from the limitations we build around us. I wondered if there will come a time when we will live in harmony with the environment or whether we will ultimately destroy everything we hold dear. I hoped that the notions of truth and freedom can one day be a reality in the hearts and minds of people everywhere.

A few minutes later there was only the subtle glow of a candle lighting my bedroom. I lay there for what seemed like hours just thinking about what had happened. I thought of my own transformation from the boy on the streets of London to the man that I was now.

Ultimately I considered the philosophy of benevolence I have outlined in this book. This highlights the situations in our world that are not just wrong, but that call on us to act out of our sense of humanity and spiritual understanding. Many live in poverty to the point of lacking even their basic needs. Imagine this situation in modern Europe; it would never be tolerated. The world would act without question. Yet we live in a world where many suffer and die with little to no reaction from the governments and peoples of the world. Most of us in the Western world have wealth enough to make a difference to these situations. If we choose we can go without the unnecessary products that dominate our lifestyles and give to a charity or project working to alleviate suffering. We can volunteer and seek out ways to raise awareness of the world's exploited and ignored.

Compassion and spiritual awareness mean little if we are not compelled by them to act in some way to create change. This is the real meaning of a philosophy of benevolence; it is a philosophy of action, change and growth. It is about extending our compassion to the four corners of the globe, to the places of greatest need. Through compassion and empathic awareness we gain from an understanding of the Golden Rule, from spiritual experiences and from seeing ourselves reflected in others we change our world. In every human and non-human life we see reflected an aspect of potential harmony; it is only by communicating this to others that we spread the understanding of life.

Every action we take should help us to see the interconnections in life and to stand with resolve and truth against inhumanity.

In this way we fulfil our potential to be more than we thought possible, on a personal level, and also in our many varied relationships in the world. This book has been an illustration of my journey so far, based upon not only the experiences of my life, but how those experiences have transformed and influenced me. I hope that within that journey you can see the outlines of a philosophy, a view of life rooted in both the upheavals of life and the spiritual heights. In every colour, sound, feeling and in every word we encounter during our lives there is a depth, an initiation into a new stage in the potential of life.

When I stand looking back over the first three decades of my life, I experience an overwhelming feeling of gratitude for the privilege I have been given. I sense a spiritual transformation like a revolution of the heart. I see in each of my abilities and experiences a glimpse of something as old as humanity, something as human as our searching for love and our desire for family and ultimately community. Where these ideas will take us in the future I don't know. I can only hope that as humanity grows and transforms it will remember to embrace the full spectrum of human experience and to remember the importance of, above all things, living with freedom from arbitrary limitations, with an enquiring desire to learn and explore and ultimately an awakening from a state of unconscious apathy to a state of peace born of awareness.

Footnotes

1. Robert Monroe was a famous explorer of the OBE state and the author of several books including the classic '*Journeys Out of the Body*'.

2. Psi is a *neutral* scientific term for extrasensory perception and other anomalous or unexplained phenomena.

3. Ingo Swann is a renowned psychic or 'perception researcher' as he prefers to be known, and is one of the key developers of remote viewing a modern term for a form of controlled clair-voyance.

BOOKS

O is a symbol of the world, of oneness and unity. In different cultures it also means the "eye," symbolizing knowledge and insight. We aim to publish books that are accessible, constructive and that challenge accepted opinion, both that of academia and the "moral majority."

Our books are available in all good English language bookstores worldwide. If you don't see the book on the shelves ask the bookstore to order it for you, quoting the ISBN number and title. Alternatively you can order online (all major online retail sites carry our titles) or contact the distributor in the relevant country, listed on the copyright page.

See our website www.o-books.net for a full list of over 500 titles, growing by 100 a year.

And tune in to myspiritradio.com for our book review radio show, hosted by June-Elleni Laine, where you can listen to the authors discussing their books.

MySpiritRadio